COSMIC SPARKS

I read with interest and delight Margie Abbott's series of rituals. The rituals capture in an involving, extending and accurate fashion the teaching of Pope Francis in *Laudato Si'*. The rituals are faithful to the teaching of the Church and make exemplary use of contemporary songs and ecologically inspired writing.

Tony Densley, formerly University of South Australia

Using a variety of well-known spiritual teachers and leaders, Margie Abbott has here compiled a deeply spiritual and experiential invitation into the most urgent issue of our time: relating to the elements of Earth. This book reflects the spiritual unfolding that is drawing people closer to the divine nature of elemental creation, and offers specific and concrete ways to engage mind, heart and body with the Cosmos herself.

Brenda Peddigrew, RSM (NL), Canada

With a stunning richness of resources, these rituals call heart and body into the profound mystery of soul –not of human beings alone, but of the Earth herself, with her accompanying elements of Air, Water and Fire. All the manifestations of grounded reality are here in one place, enough for years of learning to relate to our complex, cosmic world. Through this book, Margie Abbott RSM is offering a detailed and practical resource that anyone can use to enter into a physical, heart-centred and nurturing relationship with the Earth. This work is desperately needed in our precarious world, as the Earth signals increasing distress in escalating ways.

Brenda Peddigrew RSM (NL. Canada)
Writer, Facilitator, Teacher

A tremendous gift – an easy to use resource, full of unique depth, meaning and beauty for those of us engaged in facilitating prayer and ritual in many settings for the challenges of our times. I can't wait to use this book with my groups!

This book is a generous sharing of years of experience of creating rituals with the language, symbols and actions that resonate with us all now, sorely needed at this time of Earth's distress and human suffering. These rituals have the potential to awaken the shift in consciousness needed for our times.

The ground-breaking rituals contained in this book offer us the experiences we need as reminders that we humans participate in a single, sacred community. Margie's work gives us opportunities to awaken anew to this reality, using both traditional and contemporary practices, that we may be inspired to imaginative action to love, heal and restore Earth.

A weaving of meaning from the great traditions is brought to new relevance in light of our awakening to the Story of the Universe. The language, symbols and imagery are carefully chosen to express the new reality of our times, giving us ways to gather together to celebrate Earth's sacred depths, our gratitude for Earth's gifts, and to share our despair for Earth's destruction.

In order for us humans to grasp the enormity and implications of the Universe Story, we need constant reminders for it all to sink in. These rituals provide an opportunity for groups to express the sacred depths we encounter in the Earth community, to take up the challenges of our times in imaginative ways, and to deal with the grief we share that may otherwise leave us frozen.

Sally Neaves, Rahamim Ecological Centre, Bathurst

Margie Abbott has constructed these rituals mainly for group use, but may just as easily provide an excellent ground for personal meditation. When done in either mode, the nature and construction of the rituals keeps the individual or the group in touch with the wider sacred Earth community, using the four elements Fire, Earth, Air and Water as major points of reference. Each ritual makes reference to two or three sources for reflective quotes and poetry, and in doing calls upon a wide variety of traditional sources such as Scripture and indigenous wisdoms, as well as current thinkers on cosmology and Earth-based spirituality.

The rituals are also very earthed and practical, inviting participants to use the various senses of touch, hearing, seeing and smell to immerse themselves in a body-soul experience. Margie also sets up the rituals for use by groups that might meet regularly, inviting participants to prepare for each ritual in a number of ways.

The rituals are very contemporary, addressing issues such as Earth degradation, and other issues affecting the individual or humanity as a whole. There rituals are an excellent source for personal or group transformation at a time when we are crying out for meaningful ways to nurture the spirit.

Trevor Parton, formerly Glenburn Ecological Centre

IGNITING
A RE-ENCHANTMENT
WITH THE SACRED

COSMIC SPARKS

MARGIE ABBOTT RSM

COVENTRY
PRESS

Published in Australia by
Coventry Press
33 Scoresby Road
Bayswater Vic. 3153
Australia

ISBN 9780648566199

Copyright © Institute Property Association Limited 2020

All rights reserved. Other than for the purposes and subject to the conditions prescribed under the *Copyright Act*, no part of this publication may be reproduced, stored in a retrieval system, or transmitted in any form or by any means, electronic, mechanical, photocopying, recording or otherwise, without the prior permission of the publisher.

Scripture quotations are from the *New Revised Standard Version Bible*, copyright 1989, Division of Christian Education of the National Council of the Churches of Christ in the United States of America. Used by permission. All rights reserved.

Cataloguing-in-Publication entry is available from the National Library of Australia http:/catalogue.nla.gov.au/.

Cover image by Kristiana Prasetyo, sgm
Cover design by Ian James - www.jgd.com.au
Text design by Megan Low (Film Shot Graphics FSG)

Typeset in Adobe Garamond size 11 on 16pts
Printed in Australia

Dedicated to David Charles Lovell (1944-2018)
Renowned Publisher and Dear Friend

CONTENTS

FOREWORD 11
INTRODUCTION 13
LIST OF ACKNOWLEDGMENTS. 15
   SONGS 15
   YOUTUBES 15
   POEMS 16
   WEBSITES 16

EARTH RITUALS
RECONCILIATION 20
EARTH RITUAL. 21
LAUDATO SI': The Encyclical of Pope Francis on the Environment 22
EARTH IDENTITY. 23
A PRAYER FOR OUR EARTH: Pope Francis (adapted) 24
WELCOME WINTER. 25
A WINTER MANDALA 26
PRAYING WITH MANTRAS IN WINTER 27
EARTH MEDITATION. 28
EARTH 29
VOLCANO SUNDAY 30
EARTHQUAKE SUNDAY. 31
COMMUNITY EARTH RITUAL: WINTER SOLSTICE 32
A WINTER LAMENT: "CARING FOR OUR COMMON HOME". 33
AN EARTH MEDITATION MANDALA 34
THE OFFERING: TEILHARD DE CHARDIN 35
INTERBEING AND INTERCONNECTION. 36
EARTH LAMENT. 38
FOREST SUNDAY 39
WHERE YOU ARE STANDING IS HOLY GROUND 40
JESUS TREADS CONSCIOUSLY. 41
HOLDING THE GAZE 42

AIR RITUALS
RECONCILIATION 44
CREATIVE INTENTIONING 45
BREATH. 46
ATMOSPHERE SUNDAY. 48

JESUS IN THE FRESH AIR	49
A GROUP SPRING RITUAL: THE LILAC TREE	50
A SPRING CONTEMPLATIVE POEM	52
A MINDFULNESS WALK	53
REVERENCING ALL LIFE: A MORNING WALK	54
COMMUNITY EARTH RITUAL: SPRING EQUINOX	55
SPIRIT PRESENT IN ALL THAT IS	56
EXAMEN of CONSCIOUSNESS	58
MANTRAS: A SPRINGTIME MEDITATON	60
STARGAZING IN SPRING	61
SKY SUNDAY REFLECTION	62
AN ANCIENT PRAYER	63
THE BEATITUDES AS INSPIRED BY THE ORIGINAL ARAMAIC	64
LAUDATO SI': AIR	65
INVOKING THE ELEMENT AIR	66
CLIMATE EMERGENCY	67
PEACE	68
A MEDITATION ON AIR	69
EXTINCTION OF SPECIES: A SORROWFUL MOMENT IN TIME	70
BREATHE LOVE	71

WATER RITUALS

WALKING MEDITATION FOR RECONCILIATION	74
A MEDITATION ON PRESENCE	75
COSMIC WALK	76
COMMUNITY EARTH RITUAL: SUMMER SOLSTICE	77
THE CLOUDS	78
OCEAN SUNDAY	80
I AM A SPRING	82
A LITANY FOR BIRDS	83
WE GIVE THANKS	84
JESUS BY THE LAKE	85
STONE FLOWS TO WATER	86
PROTECTING THE WATER BODIES OF THE WORLD	88
SUMMER MANDALA	89
CARING FOR OUR COMMON HOME	90
INVOKING THE FOUR ELEMENTS	92
FALLING IN LOVE WITH EARTH	93
NEW STORY IN SONG	94

LITANY OF GRIEF... 95
EVOLVING UNIVERSE... 96
HEART ATTUNEMENT WITH ALL THAT IS... 97
RIVER SUNDAY: WORLD RIVERS DAY (4th Sunday in September)... 98
UNIVERSE IS SACRED... 100

FIRE RITUALS
RECONCILIATION... 102
A MEDITATION ON LOVE... 103
THE FIRE... 104
IGNITING SPARKS: GREETING THE DAWN... 106
COMMUNITY EARTH RITUAL: AUTUMN EQUINOX... 107
BUSHFIRE SUNDAY... 108
ROUND TABLES JUSTICE REFLECTION RITUAL... 109
WALKING FOR HOPE... 110
JESUS BY THE FIRE... 112
MINDFULNESS IN AUTUMN... 113
MANTRAS: AN AUTUMN MEDITATON... 114
CONVERSION AND ACTION NOW: CLIMATE EMERGENCY... 115
INFINITE BEAUTY... 116
WAY OF BEAUTY... 117
WAY OF BLESSING AND AFFIRMATION:... 118
A MEDITATION WITH OILS... 118
AN AUTUMN MANDALA... 119
BLESSING OF THE ANIMALS SUNDAY... 120
THE IN BETWEEN LIGHT... 122
EARTH DAY... 124
BIBLICAL PRAYERS (adapted)... 125
CELEBRATING EIGHTH WORK OF MERCY... 126
COSMIC SPARKS... 127
BIBLIOGRAPHY... 128

FOREWORD

We worship as we believe

Lex Orandi, Lex Credendi is a motto of the Catholic faith. It means that worship leads belief and that good liturgy is essential for all our lives. Unfortunately, this has not happened in the history of the liturgy in the Catholic Church. In recent centuries, some of the theology behind our liturgy is often far removed from the values of the Gospel of Jesus, especially in the lack of respect for God's earth.

Now with Pope Francis' encyclical *Laudato Si'* (On Care for Our Common Home), we can make a new start. St Francis' beautiful canticle "*Laudato Si', mi' Signore,*" reminds us that our common home is like a sister with whom we share our life and a beautiful mother who opens her arms to embrace us. It would be nice to suppose that the vision of St Francis, especially his relationship with all creation, had continued and blossomed during the centuries after his death. Unfortunately, this did not happen. In fact, the opposite occurred; the creation-centred focus of Francis' vision was lost, even among the Franciscans. In the wake of the Black Death (1346-1352), a pessimistic, anti-world mood spread throughout Europe and was adopted by the Roman Liturgy. The negative attitude to creation was endemic in the missal of Pope Pius V, which was used right up to the Second Vatican Council. The post-communion prayer during Advent read as follows, "*Oremus, Domine, doceas nos terrena despicere, et amare celestia*" ("*Let us pray, Lord, teach us to despise the things of earth, and to love the things of heaven.*")

Because of this anti-matter stance, the formal liturgy of the Eucharist has failed to recognise the energising power which good, imaginative liturgy might have in transforming the way Christians might relate to other human beings and the rest of creation. Paragraph 236 of *Laudato Si' On Care for Our Common Home* speaks of the Eucharist as an act of cosmic love. This could have made a wonderful Eucharistic prayer.

The great value of Margaret Abbott's book *Cosmic Sparks: Igniting a Re-Enchantment with the Sacred* is that she is not afraid of matter or other creatures. She creates many different liturgies that widen our experience beyond our current exclusively human-focus of the Roman Missal. There is an Earth Liturgy that acknowledges our Earth in all her fragility and beauty and allows us to give thanks for her generous gifts which supports life for both humans and all living beings. What an important liturgy this is for our time, where human activity is causing the extinction of so many of God's creatures. A recent United Nations report claims that the Earth's life support system is at crisis point as we risk causing the extinction of a million species in a few short decades.

Another Earth Liturgy begins around a clay bowl of earth which is placed in the centre of the gathering space. This liturgy invites us to embrace the ideas of extraordinary complexity involved in such words as earth, soil, dirt, ground and land. This powerful liturgy ends with everyone taking a little earth and, in silence, scattering it outside as we remember our precious earth and give thanks for her gifts.

This book will enrich the lives of Christians in both the school environment and faith communities wherever people are attempting to practise the new values that are articulated in *Laudato Si'*. Paragraph 64 tells us that "Christians realise that their responsibility with creation, and their duty towards nature and the Creator, are an essential part of their faith." Regrettably, very few Christians realise that our duty towards nature and the Creator is an essential part of our faith. We need to educate and catechise ourselves on this very vital issue. These liturgies will go a long way in helping us to do this in a way that is not possible by depending exclusively on the prayers and liturgies in the Roman Missal.

Personally, I learnt so much about nature and the environment during my time as missionary among the T'boli people on the island of Mindanao in the Philippines. If I was there now, I would love to join them in celebrating the Liturgy on Volcano Sunday.

I think that these liturgies will be used in the new Seasons of Creation which is being held in many Churches during the four or five Sundays before the Feast of St Francis on October 4th each year. With these liturgies, *Lex Orandi*, will, once again become, *Lex Credendi*.

Sean McDonagh, 2019

INTRODUCTION

Cosmic Sparks: Igniting a Re-Enchantment with the Sacred first emerged as an idea for a book of rituals when Pope Francis published *Laudato Si'* in June 2015.

In the encyclical *Laudato Si'*, Pope Francis, shows the grave consequences of our blindness to the sacred, living earth: 'Laudato Si', mi' Signor" –"Praise be to you, my Lord." In the words of his beautiful canticle, Saint Francis of Assisi reminds us that our common home is like a sister with whom we share our life and a beautiful mother who opens her arms to embrace us. "Praise be to you, my Lord, through our Sister, Mother Earth, who sustains and governs us, and who produces various fruits with coloured flowers and herbs." This sister now cries out to us because of the harm we have inflicted on her by our irresponsible use and abuse of the goods with which God has endowed her. We have come to see ourselves as her lords and masters, entitled to plunder her at will … We have forgotten that we ourselves are dust of the earth; our very bodies are made up of her elements, we breathe her air and we receive life and refreshment from her waters.' (LS: 2015 1-2)

This ritual book is building on the thesis that Earth is all we have; we come from Earth and unto Earth we shall return. This book is about realising that Earth is sacred once and for all. Earth is under stress and in the words of Elizabeth Johnson, "Ecological Conversion means falling in love with earth as an inherently valuable, living community in which we participate, and bending every effort to be creatively faithful to its well-being, in tune with the living God who brought it into being and cherishes it with unconditional love." (Elizabeth Johnson 2014: 259)

Quotes from theologians and writers cited on each page of the book emphasise the interrelationship with Pope Francis' work, the need for new rituals and liturgies, and openness to ecological conversion.

I am influenced by Sean McDonagh saying in the *National Catholic Reporter* in May 2016 that things need to change liturgically, the church "would start to begin creating prayers and liturgies that support this new engagement and new spirituality and new ethics with creation." *Cosmic Sparks* is a contribution towards bringing this dream to life.

In addition, I am also challenged by John F. Haught who teaches that the cosmos is unfolding, and, like Thomas Berry, places the Universe Story at the heart – prayer and ritual celebrating these phenomena "can only wait patiently and attentively, without forcing our will on the flow of time." (Haught 2017:200)

Cosmic Sparks is in four parts with each quarter attributed to one of the four elements: earth, air, fire and water. The rituals can be adapted to suit your needs and are written for indoor and outdoor use as well as silent contemplation or with a group. Every ritual begins with contemplative silence, an Acknowledgment of Country and concludes in silence. If resources are required, they are mentioned in the beginning of the ritual. Songs, YouTubes and Poems will be acknowledged elsewhere in the book.

For anyone new to this kind of ritual, I suggest that you change the times for silence to suit yourself and adapt the ritual to create mindfulness and contemplation that works for you. The main reason for this book is to enter into relationship with Earth and the interconnectedness of all that is.

I particularly want to thank Sean McDonagh for the Foreword; Trevor Parton for helping me name the book; Brenda Peddigrew RSM, Sally Neaves, Tony Densley and Trevor Parton for the endorsements. Many thanks also to proof readers – Tricia Gimpel, Philippa Lovell, Julie O'Brien RSM and Cathy Solano RSM.

Norm Habel and Diarmuid O'Murchu kindly gave me permission to adapt their prayers and I am very grateful.

The beautiful cover is painted by Kristiana Prasetyo, sgm, a member of the Green Mountain Monastery, Vermont. This community was co-founded with Thomas Berry. Kristiana also works for Eco Learning Camp, Bandung, Indonesia. Deep thanks to Kris.

I am also very grateful to Jan Novotka, John Seed, Joanna Macey, Mary Southard, David Suzuki, Marian McClelland, Helen Densley, Trevor Parton, Carmel Crameri, Jim Casey, Brenda Peddigrew, Michael Morwood, Elizabeth Young, Colleen Rhodes, Adele Howard, Neil Davidson, Helen Kearins, Gabrielle Sinclair, Loretta Brinkman and Pat O'Gorman for allowing me to use their original works.

Several friends prayed many of the rituals and gave me valuable feedback for improvement. I thank them.

Jen Callanan and I intended to write this book together. It became evident that our audiences were different. *Cosmic Sparks* is oriented towards adults and spiritual seekers whilst Jen's book is more oriented to young people and children. Jen's book is entitled *Sparks of the Universe*: Prayers and Rituals for young people and adolescents embracing the spirit of *Laudato Si'* and Ecological Conversion.

During the writing of this book, I was in communication with Daniel O'Leary, the prolific and creative writer from Ireland, who died in January 2019. He wrote: "I wish you every blessing in this vital work. It all marks a huge shift and refocus for a radical new beginning for our church and for the meaning of Incarnation." (September 2019)

"The world is, therefore, a web of relationships and we humans and all creation are in movement toward God. The more humans enter into relationships, the more we live in communion with God. Everything is interconnected." (LS: 240)

We are in dangerous times because climate emergency is upon us. Ecological Conversion is needed and I hope that these prayers and rituals will birth a re-enchantment with the sacred that furthers a strong web of relationships that builds a sustainable future for all.

Margie Abbott RSM

LIST OF ACKNOWLEDGMENTS
SONGS, POEMS AND YOUTUBES

SONGS
Bob Randall and Christine Morrison *Kanyini Chant*
Jan Novotka *Within All; The Presence You Are; Earth our Home; Consciousness Waking; Dust Alive; In the Name of all That Is; Creative Contemplation; Earth Community; Could it Be; Sacred Fire; Walk Lightly*
Susan Lincoln and Craig Toungate, *Aramaic Lord's Prayer; Like a Feather on the Breath of God*
Sarah Thomsen *By Breath; Deep Peace*
Helen Kearins RSM: *Bringing Them Home; Round Tables*
Alicia Bonnet and the New Moon Singers, *Mother I Feel You Under My Feet*
Melissa Phillipe *There is Only One of Us;*
Gurrumul, *Marrandil*
Kathy Sherman, *Sacred Fire*
Katie Ketchum, *Ubi Caritas*
Murray Kyle, *Unlock Your Memory; Stone Flows to Water; Circle Round; Every Moment*
Betsy Rose, *Mother Earth*
Jeff Stockton, *Beauty Before Me*
One Love Devotional Chant, *May All Beings*
Australian Nature Sounds *Early Morning Songbirds*
Dev Premal Mantras, *Om Shanti Om*
Circle of Friends, *Peace on Earth*
Aboriginal Earth Chants: *Uluru Monument to Time*
Karen Drucker: *One Breath at a Time*
Chants Ritual Music: *The Beginning of the Earth*
One Earth Chants Circle of Friends: *E Tu Kahikatea*

YOUTUBES
Peter Mayer, *My Soul* https://youtu.be/sXxfA3pyZgI,
John Seed, *Child of The Universe* https://youtu.be/wauTegRZ6KE
Sean McDonagh, *Caring for Our Common Home,* https://youtu.be/hMG59xDGZ2w
Nitin Das *India's Healing Forest Trailer* YouTube link https://youtu.be/9ohmgsh3D7c

Leonard Cohen Anthem https://youtu.be/6wRYjtvIYK0
Transition Streets Geelong Show Me How: https://youtu.be/ZyXl1DpZPLA
Dancing Sophia's Circle Just to be is a Blessing: https://youtu.be/aaAWvshg6xw
A Grateful Day:https://youtu.be/zSt7k_q_qRU
Greta Thunberg: https://youtu.be/RjsLm5PCdVQ
Greta Thunberg:https://youtu.be/KAJsdgTPJpU
Sara Thomsen: https://youtu.be/kb-FAOe396U
Carolyn McDade: https://youtu.be/cMNwYBUbXF4
Connie Barlow: https://youtu.be/DtyDxjwd7oU
Ronda La Rue and david Whyte: https://youtu.be/On7ma4UFVVM

POEMS
Carmel Crameri RSJ *The Tree*
Trevor Parton: *The Fire; Breath; the Clouds; Identity*
Helen Densley rsm *The In-Between-Light; The Brolgas; Symphony Under the Stars*
Marian McClelland, *Let Winter Wrap You Round*
Elizabeth young rsm *Morning Walk*
Brenda Peddigrew rsm *The Lilac Tree*

WEBSITES
Brenda Peddigrew rsm. (https://soulwinds.ca/brenda.html)
David Clark 2014: www.sharingculture.info
Lilac Growing in Spring,https://youtu.be/HIDIKD6eknc
Mick Dodson: https://www.reconciliation.org.au/wp-content/uploads/2017/11/Welcome-to-and-Acknowledgement-of-Country.pdf
Joanna Macy and John Seed Gaia*Meditation*, "Thinking like a Mountain – Towards a Council of All Beings" www.rainforestinfo.org.au/deep-eco/TLAM%20text.htm, Theo Simons https://en.wikipedia.org/wiki/Seize_the_Day_(band) The lyrics may be found https://lyricstranslate.com/en/rainbow-songs-child-universe-lyrics.html
Buderim Centre of Spirituality & Ecology: www.buderimspiritualityecologycentre.com
Diarmuid O'Murchu http://www.diarmuid13.com/
2018 Vatican Observatory Summer School. (https://youtu.be/0_-VIf38Cg4)
Diarmuid O'Murchu, http://www.diarmuid13.com/special-prayers.
Diarmuid O'Murchu, http://www.diarmuid13.com/special-prayers
Glenys Livingstone: Spring, Summer, Winter and Autumn Meditation https://pagaian.org/pagaian-prayers-invoking-her/
Miriam McGillis OP: The *Cosmic Walk*http://www.thegreatstory.org/CosmicWalk.pdf
Norm Habel (original work adapted) http://normanhabel.com/
The Sustainable Hour 94.7fm the Pulse Geelong

Maryknoll Office for Global Concerns https://maryknollogc.org/

Mary Southard, https://www.marysouthardart.org/blog/ My Heart Aches

Rhonda Fabian: https://www.kosmosjournal.org/kj_article/on-elevating-the-narrative/

Colleen Rhodes RSM: https://institute.mercy.org.au/wp-content/uploads/2017/11/Trinity-Heart-of-the-Cosmic-Mystery-

Australian Religious Response to Climate Change: https://www.arrcc.org.au/

Global Catholic Climate Movement: https://catholicclimatemovement.global/

Sean McDonagh:https://www.ncronline.org/

Brian Roewe: https://www.ncronline.org/

Earth Day's 50th Anniversary www.earthday.org/earthday/countdown2020

Rahamim Ecology Centre: https://www.rahamim.org.au/podcasts

Rhonda La Rue: https://www.youtube.com/rondalarue

https://www.referendumcouncil.org.au/sites/default/files/2017-05/Uluru_Statement_From_The_Heart_0.PDF

https://www.ncronline.org/

ELEMENT: EARTH

DIRECTION: SOUTH

SEASON: WINTER

GIFT: STRENGTH

Earth ~ South ~ Winter ~ Strength

RECONCILIATION

'We invite you to walk with us in a movement of the Australian people for a better future."
Uluru Statement from the Heart 2017

Background: Reconciliation is an everyday challenge. In 1998, Australia stopped to recognise for the first time a National Sorry Day – 26th May.

Sorry Day precedes National Reconciliation Week, which commences on 27th May (the anniversary of the 1967 referendum) and concludes on 3rd June (the anniversary of the 1992 Mabo judgment).

Genuine reconciliation also requires acknowledgment of the harm done by the perpetrators and beneficiaries of past policies so that healing can reach through the whole community.

Aboriginal children were removed from their parents for many years. This caused trauma, deep loss and grief. Sometimes the removal of these children is referred to as 'stealing'. There is a place for us to become more conscious of this fact by celebrating a National Sorry Day ritual.

Resource: Helen Kearins: *Bringing Them Home* streaming on Apple Music and Spotify.

Begin with three minutes of contemplative silence followed by Acknowledgment of Country.

Reflection: *But now I know the stories and*
The policies that rent their lives asunder.
Not by chance the children gone
But dread intent to clear the land of 'trouble'.
Now's the time clear our minds and listen to the truth
Only open hearts can heal the wounds that crippled youth
And only willing feet can walk together in the sand
And heal the grieving spirit of this land.

(Helen Kearins RSM)

Litany of Lament

Presider: Breathing Ancient Spirit of this Land
All: Present you have been since the beginning, now, and ever shall be. How can we forget?
Presider: For trauma, deep loss and grief; no treaty and no permission; to the First Nation's People.
All: Time to say we are sorry.
Presider: For harm done by perpetrators and beneficiaries of past policies.
All: Time to walk together.
Presider: In the name of all who have suffered injustice. Lest we forget.
All: Listen to the Stories.

Bless Australia 'the grieving spirit of this land'. Conclude with one minute of contemplative silence.

Earth ~ South ~ Winter ~ Strength

EARTH RITUAL

"**Ecological sensitivity requires a frank admission that nature is our final home and not a mere station on the human journey.**" **(John F. Haught 2015:150)**

Begin with three minutes of contemplative silence followed by Acknowledgment of Country. *Earth Our Home* Jan Novotka – Streaming Apple Music and Spotify.

Listen to the song. This ritual is best prayed outside, alone or with a group.

Leader: We acknowledge Earth in all her fragility and beauty. We give thanks for her generous giving of life so that all humans and non-humans may live. Let us remember to tread consciously with reverence and gratitude.
Voice One: We belong to the universe, not the universe to us.
Voice Two: "We cannot discover ourselves without first discovering the universe, Earth, and the imperatives of our own being. Each of these has a creative power and a vision far beyond any rational thought or cultural creation of which we are capable. Nor should we think of these as isolated from our own individual being or from the human community. We have no existence except within Earth and within the Universe."

(Thomas Berry 1988: p. 195)

Voice One: We belong to the universe, not the universe to us.
Voice Two: Blessed be Earth.
All: Blessed be Earth.
Using your senses, pause to take in your surrounds and several deep breaths.
Voice One: Blessed be wondrous spinning jewel.
All: Blessed be wondrous spinning jewel.
Voice Two: O Earth, beautiful one! O Earth, awesome and good.
All: O Earth, beautiful one! O Earth, awesome and good.
All sing: Earth, our Home.

"We live on a wondrous spinning jewel; so fragile and precious is she.
Oh Earth, beautiful one! Oh Earth, awesome and good!
Gentle planet, giving all; Oh Earth, our home!"
© 2008 by Jan Novotka's Music, LLC (ASCAP). All rights reserved.

Conclude with one minute of contemplative silence.

Earth ~ South ~ Winter ~ Strength

LAUDATO SI': THE ENCYCLICAL OF POPE FRANCIS ON THE ENVIRONMENT

"The first focus is to call human beings to respect, cherish, and stop exploiting planet earth – the home of all creation." (Sean McDonagh 2016 xiii)

Begin with three minutes of contemplative silence followed by Acknowledgment of Country.

Leader: Today we have an uninterrupted 10 minutes to sit outside amongst trees, or by a river or the ocean to contemplate quotes from Laudato Si'. Please take this book outside with you.

"The urgent challenge to protect our common home includes a concern to bring the whole human family together to seek a sustainable and integral development, for we know that things can change." LS: 13

Pause: Close your eyes and reflect – what can I do?

"Each year hundreds of millions of tons of waste are generated, much of it non-biodegradable, highly toxic and radioactive, from homes and businesses, from construction and demolition sites, from clinical, electronic and industrial sources. Earth, our home is beginning to look more and more like an immense pile of filth." LS: 21

Pause: Close your eyes and reflect – is this a surprise to me?

"Humanity is called to recognise the need for changes of lifestyle, production and consumption." LS: 23

Pause: Close your eyes and reflect – am I willing to change my lifestyle?

"There has been a tragic rise in the number of migrants seeking to flee from the growing poverty caused by environmental degradation. They are not recognised by international conventions as refugees; they bear the loss of the lives they have left behind, without enjoying any legal protection whatsoever." LS: 25

Pause: Close your eyes and reflect – how will I respond?

"Each year sees the disappearance of thousands of plant and animal species which we will never know, which our children will never see, because they have been lost forever." LS: 33

Pause: Close your eyes and reflect.

Pope Francis highlights the importance of the Sabbath, as a time of rest for everyone, and Jubilee, as a way of distributing the goods of creation. LS: 71

Pause: Close your eyes and reflect.

Leader: Open your eyes and become aware of the outside environment wherever you are and declare your intention to tread consciously and breathe in the sacredness of all that is.

During this week, intend to greet the sun each morning.

Conclude with one minute of contemplative silence.

Earth ~ South ~ Winter ~ Strength

EARTH IDENTITY

"Everything has a right to be recognised and revered. Trees have tree rights, insects have insect rights, rivers have river rights and mountains have mountain rights" (Thomas Berry 1999:5)

Begin with three minutes of contemplative silence followed by Acknowledgment of Country.

Leader: Today we will adapt *Lectio Divina* to reflect on this poem by Trevor Parton (used with permission) and as we gather in this circle let us listen to a reading of the poem.

Identity

My consciousness comes as a result of communion.
I am already a community of beings,
and each of them a self in itself;
individual, but dependent
on what comes before and after.
Made from stardust,
but depending on what I call "me".
Who is "me"?
Me is my body, Earth body, Christ body; all stars and flaring creativity.

Leader: Let us listen to the poem again and this time you will be invited to share one word that stays with you.

Identity

My consciousness comes as a result of communion.
I am already a community of beings,
and each of them a self in itself;
individual, but dependent
on what comes before and after.
Made from stardust,
but depending on what I call "me".
Who is "me"?
Me is my body, Earth body, Christ body; all stars and flaring creativity.

Leader: Let us listen to the poem for a third time and you will be invited to share a phrase that stays with you.

Leader: Let us conclude with this mantra:

All: *Made from stardust me and you; Earth in me and Earth in all. Amen.*

Conclude with one minute of contemplative silence.

Earth ~ South ~ Winter ~ Strength

A PRAYER FOR OUR EARTH:
POPE FRANCIS (ADAPTED)

"In union with all creatures, we journey through this land seeking God, for in the words of Basil the Great, 'if the world has a beginning and if it has been created, we must enquire who gave it this beginning, and who was its Creator.' Let us sing as we go. May our struggles and our concern for this planet never take away the joy of hope?" (LS: 244)

Begin with three minutes of contemplative silence followed by Acknowledgment of Country.

Presider: Great Spirit, present in the whole universe and in the smallest of creatures; all that exists is embraced in tenderness.
All: **We give thanks, Great Spirit.**
Presider: We have the power to protect life and beauty because we are already endowed with Love.
All: **For this gift we are grateful.**
Presider: Gifted with Peace we are inspired to live as sisters and brothers harming no one.
All: **Harming no one.**
Presider: Sacred Presence Within draws us to take a stand for the abandoned and forgotten of this world.
All: **For this we are grateful.**
Presider: We are inspired to protect the world and not prey on it, sow beauty not pollution and destruction.
All: **Respecting all that is as sacred.**
Presider: We accept vulnerability and limitation within ourselves and forgive the hearts of those who look only for gain at the expense of the poor and the earth.
All: **We give thanks for vulnerability and limitation.**
Presider: An infinite light awakens our desire to discover the worth of each thing, be filled with awe wonder and contemplation, to recognise that we are profoundly united with every creature.
All: **For this gift we give thanks.**
Presider: Great Spirit, for being with us each day we give thanks.
All: **Great Spirit, for being with us each day we give thanks.**
Presider: We are encouraged to persist in our struggle for justice, love and peace.
All: **We are encouraged to persist.**

Conclude with one minute of contemplative silence.

Earth ~ South ~ Winter ~ Strength

WELCOME WINTER

"Matter made from rock and soil. It, too, is pulled by the moon as the magma circulates through the planet heart and roots such molecules into biology. Earth pours through us, replacing each cell in the body every seven years. Ashes to ashes, dust to dust, we ingest, incorporate and excrete the earth, are made from earth. I am that. You are that." (Joanna Macy, Molly Young Brown, 1998:186)

A selection of winter images has been prepared, either electronically or on photographs or pictures. These are placed in the ritual space before the ritual starts.

Begin with three minutes of contemplative silence followed by Acknowledgment of Country.

Leader: Today we have a selection of images that depict winter in the southern hemisphere. As you select one reflect on the questions I mindfully ask.

Leader: What does this picture remind you of?

Follow this reflection with sharing in small groups using a contemplative dialogue process. Each person in turn speaks of their experience and there are no interruptions or questions of clarification as the main purpose is to listen actively to the person and her/his memory. When all have finished there is a small time to reflect and then the next question is asked.

Leader: What words or images are evoked?

Follow this reflection with sharing in small groups using a contemplative dialogue process as outlined above.

Leader: What is my relationship with earth?

Follow this reflection with sharing in small groups using a contemplative dialogue process as outlined above.

Leader: What does winter mean for me?

Follow this reflection with sharing in small groups using a contemplative dialogue process as outlined above.

Leader: What are my best memories of winter?

Follow this reflection with sharing in small groups using a contemplative dialogue process as outlined above.

Leader: 'Let the winter wrap you round
Know yourself as winter's guest
Feel the touch of gentle rest
Hibernation is profound.'
Marian McClelland (used with permission)
Conclude with one minute of contemplative silence.

Earth ~ South ~ Winter ~ Strength

A WINTER MANDALA

"Everything in the universe is genetically cousin to everything else. There is literally one family, one bonding in the universe, because everything is descended from the same source.' (Thomas Berry, quoted in June: 2010)

(A circular tablecloth is placed on the floor and the group is invited to gather winter leaves from outside and then return to the room. A glass of wine and a loaf of bread are placed on another cloth beside the circular tablecloth.)
Consciousness Waking Jan Novotka – Streaming Apple Music and Spotify.

Begin with three minutes of contemplative silence followed by Acknowledgment of Country.
Leader: We give thanks for all that is, leaves of the universe raising our awareness now, honouring connectedness.
The leaves are placed on the cloth in silence to create the winter mandala.
When the mandala is complete, all gather in a circle and contemplate in silence.
We give thanks for the bread and wine, gifts of sun, seed, water and the work of human hands.
All sing: *Consciousness Waking*

Consciousness waking, holy and whole; creation stirring, birthing anew!
Now is the time! We are the space for the Holy to rise in our midst.

Consciousness waking, holy and whole; creation stirring, birthing anew!
Now is the time! We are the space for the Holy to rise in our midst.

Consciousness waking, holy and whole; creation stirring, birthing anew!
Now is the time! We are the space for the Holy to rise in our midst.

©2006 by Jan Novotka's Music, LLC (ASCAP). All rights reserved.

Leader: We break this bread and share this wine in the name of "creation stirring, birthing anew!"
The bread is then shared with those gathered and as the bread is passed, each one says:
"Now is the time! We are the Space for the Holy to rise in our midst".
The wine is then shared with those gathered and as the wine is passed, each one says:
"Now is the time! We are the Space for the Holy to rise in our midst".
At a later time you may wish to write a list of all that arises and emerges as you listen to this song.
Conclude with one minute of contemplative silence.

Earth ~ South ~ Winter ~ Strength

PRAYING WITH MANTRAS IN WINTER

"Challenges abound! How can we change the language and imagery of spiritual practices and religious rituals to honour the truth of kinship and inclusiveness?" (*Earthsong Journal*, Anne Boyd 2013:19)

"… it needs to find expression in church liturgies and Eucharistic prayers, in religious art and music, in public preaching and teaching, and in private prayers and spirituality, and devotional writing." (Elizabeth Johnson 2018:226)

Sit outside. Begin with three minutes of contemplative silence followed by Acknowledgment of Country.

Mindfully breathe in and out for several minutes and then slowly take each mantra and read it; close your eyes and repeat it to yourself accentuating the seven syllables.

Spirit of Life and Love Now

Spirit of Life and Love Now

Spirit Active in Me Now

Spirit Active in Me Now

Calling Me to Love Anew

Calling Me to Love Anew

Breathing in and Breathing Out

Breathing in and Breathing Out

Treading Consciously in Earth

Treading Consciously in Earth

Walk mindfully for 5 minutes repeating slowly the mantras.

Return to your seat outside and contemplate the words of this prayer to conclude this reflection. "Radiant Love, present in the universe since time began – from the initial flaring forth to the convergence of galaxies, from the distant stars to Earth our Common Home. I am grateful for all Earth has given me life, sustenance, creative imagination and consciousness. Spirit of Life and Love, now breathe in and breathe out anew." (Judy Cannato 2006:79 adapted).

Conclude with one minute of contemplative silence.

Earth ~ South ~ Winter ~ Strength

EARTH MEDITATION

"**Astronomer Karl Sagan maintained that people will save the planet only if they recognise it is as sacred.**" (*Earthsong Journal,* **Peter Faulkner 2005:19**)

Begin with three minutes of contemplative silence followed by Acknowledgment of Country. Take this page outside to a quiet reflective place and take some time for some deep breaths and listen to the sounds around you. Read the poem to yourself and then out aloud, repeating each line twice.

Wind and Bobwhite

    Wind and bobwhite
    And the afternoon sun
    By ceasing to question the sun
    I have become light,
    Bird and wind.
    My leaves sing.
    I am earth, earth
    All these lighted things
    Grow from my heart.
    A tall spare pine
    Stands like the initial of my first
    Name when I had one.
    When I had a spirit,
    When I was on fire
    When this valley was
    Made out of fresh air
    You spoke my name
    In naming Your silence:
    O sweet irrational worship!
    I am earth, earth…

(Thomas Merton 1967 *Selected Poems*)

Create your own prayer of gratitude for this day and for the beauty all around you.
(Feel free to conclude with Peter Mayer's song *My Soul* YouTube: https://youtu.be/sXxfA3pyZgI
Conclude with one minute of contemplative silence.

Earth ~ South ~ Winter ~ Strength

EARTH

"An eternity we thought was elsewhere now calls out to us from every cleft in every stone, from every cloud and clump of dirt. To lend our ears to the dripping glaciers – to come awake to the voices of the silence – is to be turned inside out, discovering to our astonishment that the wholeness and holiness we'd been dreaming our way towards has been holding us all along, that the secret and the sacred One that moves behind all the many traditions is none other than this animate immensity that enfolds us, this spherical eternity, glimpsed at last in its unfathomable wholeness and complexity, in its sensitivity and its sentience." (David Abram 2010: 180-181)

A clay bowl of earth is placed in the centre of the gathering space. This ritual begins inside and finishes outside.

Begin with three minutes of contemplative silence followed by Acknowledgment of Country.

(When everyone is present and still, invite people to close their eyes and listen to the reading below and then remember a time in their lives when they felt close to the land, soil, dirt, earth or ground. (3-4 minutes)

Reader: *Earth, soil, dirt, ground, land*: these terms embrace ideas of extraordinary complexity. Hidden within them is our sense of our origins, our place, our dependence on the soil beneath our feet... What we call dirt today, in the wisdom of tongue's history, is the fertile ground, the tended source of food, the planet's life... *Ground* is something solid, the space we gain or lose in battle, the place where we take a stand, the basis for all good arguments, the foundation on which we lay our buildings. *Land* denotes place or context – it means the nation or the region we belong to, as well as the part that belongs to us; it is a place of safety – we long for dry land, look for a landing place. (David Suzuki: 1997: 78)

(In twos and threes, people are then invited to share times when they felt close to land, soil, dirt or ground.)

Song: *Mother I feel you under my feet* – Alicia Bonnet and the New Moon Singers – streaming Apple Music and Spotify.

The clay bowl of earth is now taken outside in procession and a circle is created around the clay bowl. Each person takes a little piece of the earth from the cloth and in silence scatters it outside, promising to remember to be conscious of how precious earth is and to be mindful of all that we are given daily.

After the earth is scattered, the group creates a circle and breathes 5 Sufi earth breaths (in through the nose and out through the nose.)

The song is replayed and everyone joins in *Mother I feel you under my feet*.

Conclude with one minute of contemplative silence.

Earth ~ South ~ Winter ~ Strength

VOLCANO SUNDAY

"There is a large skylight above my head and in the predawn darkness I can see the shining stars of the Milky Way Galaxy. The words of the psalmist come to mind 'Praise God, sun and moon; praise God, shining stars!' The luminous fire that burned in those stars has burned through 15 billion years of Universe unfolding and burns in me this morning. It burns in my hunger for the Holy." (*Earthsong Journal*, Gail Worcelo 2000:10)

"The mountains and the hills before you will burst into song." (Isaiah 55:12)

(Adapted with permission http://normanhabel.com/)

Begin with three minutes of contemplative silence followed by Acknowledgment of Country.

Leader: Today we acknowledge volcanoes and volcanic forces. We sing with the rocks and depths of Earth. We celebrate the underground presence of nature. We connect with the mystery of volcanoes that connect us in turn with vibrant mysteries deep in planet earth.

Leader: We invite volcanoes to join us in wonder:

All: Red molten rocks waiting deep down below, hot boiling lava ready to flow.

Leader: We join with mountain creatures in praising God.

All: Wild forest animals sensing the danger, leaving the scene and trembling with fear.

Leader: We call volcanic soils to celebrate:

All: Ancient fertile lands rich in flora, precious gems and rich red ore.

Reader: Exodus 19:16-23

(*If we accept that Earth is the result of violent eruptions in the cosmos – from the time of the first big bang – then volcanic eruptions are an extension of the impulses God has planted in creation from the beginning. Yes, volcanoes are part of God's continuing creation. That does not mean we should ignore that Christ, who became an Earth being for us, will always empathise with any who suffer because of these eruptions.*)

All: As we view volcanoes, we have a sense of fear as well as wonder. We see evidence of the deep powerful forces planted in creation as wondrous and natural. May we recognise that volcanoes too are alive with your Spirit and to rejoice with all the forces of the wild. As we revere Earth, we do so in the name of Great Spirit who reconciles and renews all things in creation. Amen.

Conclude with one minute of contemplative silence.

Earth ~ South ~ Winter ~ Strength

EARTHQUAKE SUNDAY

"…These will include the close relationship between the poor and our fragile planet: the belief that we are all connected; the way in which we understand economics, technology, and progress; the belief that every person has dignity; the truly serious need for an international policy; and the need for honest dialogue about how to proceed, imagining a new and more sustainable lifestyle for all. (LS: 16)

(Adapted with permission http://normanhabel.com/)

Begin with three minutes of contemplative silence followed by Acknowledgment of Country.

Leader: We take time today to recall recent earthquakes and tsunamis on planet earth. We recall all who suffer in such disasters, humans, rocks, soil, fauna and flora as well as animals.

Leader: Contemplating all that is

All: when we hear of the hidden plates of Earth moving and quaking beneath us, we tremble in awe and fear for all those suffering.

Leader: Contemplating all that is

All: when fault lines begin to move in different parts of the world, we tremble in awe and fear.

Leader: Contemplating all that is

All: when earthquakes trigger a tsunami and walls of water flood the shore we remember those affected.

Leader: Contemplating all that is

All: when shorelines are battered and homes washed out to sea our hearts break with compassion for all who suffer.

Leader: Contemplating all that is

All: we pray that our fragile planet will benefit from human beings taking steps towards a "new and worldwide solidarity of will and talent to care for God's creation". (LS: 14)

Reader: Matthew 25:45

Leader: As we remember earthquakes and tsunamis, we have a sense of compassion as well as fear. We begin to see the deep powerful forces planted in creation as wondrous and natural, but also forces to face with fear.

All: We believe Great Spirit renews life in creation and groans in empathy with a suffering creation.

Conclude with one minute of contemplative silence.

Earth ~ South ~ Winter ~ Strength

COMMUNITY EARTH RITUAL: WINTER SOLSTICE

"In *Canticle of the Cosmos*, Brian Swimme says that every child should be told this: 'You come out of the energy that gave birth to the universe. Its story is your story; its beginning is your beginning.' Children's hearts will recognise these wondrous words, and will soon learn to protect and to nourish the loving, evolving heart of their Divine Mother Earth."
(Daniel O'Leary 2018: 163)

This is a link to Glenys Livingstone's website and there you can purchase the winter meditation https://pagaian.org/pagaian-prayers-invoking-her/

A Possible Process for Creating a Ritual – Remote Preparation

For several years, a community group has been meeting to welcome winter and create a ritual together.

Two weeks before the scheduled ritual, an email is sent to the group to remind them to reflect on winter and allow their contemplative stance to flow freely.

"For those of you who are coming for the first time we have been working with the idea of a 'contemplative stance' – allowing anything that emerges in us as winter nears - thought; idea; action; musing; daydreaming; synchronicity, etc. So make a note and bring something to celebrate this at the winter solstice ritual.

We will celebrate with whatever you bring to contribute to the ritual – out of your reflections since the last ritual – poetry; music; sacred space décor; symbols; readings; movement; drama, dance; and art works."

Suggested Process for Creating Ritual on the Day

Gather in a circle and acknowledge the land and original ancestors.

Begin with three minutes of contemplative silence.

The leader invites each person one by one to share what they have brought to the ritual.

The listening process is discerning and appreciative.

Using contemplative listening (one person speaks at a time and whatever is suggested is accepted without interruption or disagreement), the group then suggests possible placing and timing of the texts, décor, music, dance, etc. This usually works out smoothly and with great respect for the gifts shared among the group.

The ritual is enacted.

Conclude with one minute of contemplative silence.

Lunch follows.

Earth ~ South ~ Winter ~ Strength

A WINTER LAMENT: "CARING FOR OUR COMMON HOME"

"Our current way of thinking about how we extract resources from the earth is based on a fundamental lie. The lie is that there is an infinite supply of earth's goods. The lie leads us to believe that we can squeeze the earth dry and somehow – magically– it will renew itself." (LS: 106)

Begin with three minutes of contemplative silence followed by Acknowledgment of Country. Afterwards, watch this YouTube on caring for Our Common Home with Sean McDonagh https://youtu.be/hMG59xDGZ2w

Leader: We gather today to lament the pain we are inflicting on Earth. "It is an extraordinary and awesome moment in human and earth affairs that the behaviour of one or two generations can have such a profound and irreversible impact, not just on human history but on the planet as well." (Sean McDonagh 2016:35)

All: How long must I bear this pain in my soul and live with sorrow all the day? (Nan Merrill 2007:17)

Voice One: We consciously invoke element earth in this season of winter, and recall the grounding powers from which we can draw strength in adversity. We lament the misuse of Earth's gifts.

All: How long must I bear this pain in my soul and live with sorrow all the day? (Nan Merrill 2007:17) We lament the misuse of earth's gifts.

Voice Two: We consciously and reverently invoke element air, and recall the inspiring power of air from which we can draw the gift of truth. We lament the pollution and poisoning of air.

All: How long must I bear this pain in my soul and live with sorrow all the day? (Nan Merrill 2007:17) We lament the pollution and poisoning of air.

Voice Three: We consciously invoke the element of water, and recall the creative powers of water from which we can draw love. We lament the dumping of toxic waste into our waterways.

All: How long must I bear this pain in my soul and live with sorrow all the day? (Nan Merrill 2007:17) We lament the dumping of toxic waste into our waterways.

Voice Four: We consciously invoke the element of fire, and recall the shaping powers of fire from which we can draw beauty. We lament the effects of climate change and the raging bushfires across Earth.

All: How long must I bear this pain in my soul and live with sorrow all the day? (Nan Merrill 2007:17) We lament the effects of climate change and the raging bushfires across Earth.

Conclude with one minute of contemplative silence.

Earth ~ South ~ Winter ~ Strength

AN EARTH MEDITATION MANDALA

"Thus, the creatures of this world no longer appear to us under merely natural guise because the risen One is mysteriously holding them to himself and directing them towards fullness as their end. The very flowers of the field and the birds which his human eyes contemplated and admired are now imbued with his radiant presence." (LS: 100)

This ritual is best done in a quiet place where you can create a mandala. A mandala is a circular shape that can be made with coloured pencils; crayons; fruit; seeds; or coloured rice.

Begin with three minutes of contemplative silence followed by Acknowledgment of Country.

Play *Early Morning Songbirds* – or any birdsong of your choice streaming on apple Music and Spotify.

Read this poem by Helen Densley RSM as you warm up to creating your mandala.

Symphony Under The Stars

>Sound
>breaks through
>explodes
>like
>fire works
>in the
>night sky
>I am
>lifted up
>to the place
>where the music
>lives
>in colour's beauty
>caressed within
>music's mandala
>
>>(used with permission)

A Calming Breath Meditation

Calm your mind and let go any tension.
It helps to tense different body parts and let them go.
Feel yourself surrounded by peace and serenity.
Breathe in peace and breathe out peace.
Create your mandala whilst listening to the birdsong.
Conclude with one minute of contemplative silence.

Earth ~ South ~ Winter ~ Strength

THE OFFERING: TEILHARD DE CHARDIN

"As we become planetary species by our physical presence and environmental impact, we need also to become planetary species by our expansion of comprehensive compassion to all life forms." (Arthur Fabel, Donald St John 2003:7)

(Adapted for the 21st century with inclusive language.)

Song: Jan Novotka *Dust Alive* – streaming Apple Music and Spotify.

Begin with three minutes of contemplative silence followed by Acknowledgment of Country.

Reflection: In *Laudato Si'*, Pope Francis reminds us that "we humans… must take our place within creation, not stand outside it in a superior position. It is a distorted view of human life that claims we are better or more important than the rest of creation… each created animal or plant reflects the face of God." (LS: 69)

The Offering

Today you are invited to savour the words of Teilhard De Chardin when in China he had no bread and wine and celebrated Mass on the World. (Teilhard de Chardin 1961:19)

"Since once again, though this time not in the forests of the Aisne but in the steppes of Asia – I have neither bread, nor wine, nor altar, I will raise myself beyond these symbols… I, your priest, will make the whole earth my altar and on it I will offer you all the labours and sufferings of the world.

"Over there, on the horizon, the sun has just touched with light the outermost fringe of the eastern sky. Once again, beneath this moving sheet of fire, the living surface of the earth wakes and trembles, and once again begins its fearful travail. I will place on my paten the harvest to be won by this renewal of labour. Into my chalice I shall pour all the sap which is pressed out this day from the earth's fruits.

"My paten and my chalice are the depths of soul laid widely open to all the forces which in a moment will rise up from every corner of earth and converge upon the spirit. Grant me the remembrance and the mystic presence of all those of whom the light is now awakening to the new day."

Song: *Dust Alive©2003 by Jan Novotka's Music, LLC (ASCAP). All rights reserved.*

The dust of the stars is my flesh. The dust of the stars is my blood. Oh, the dust of stars holds the gift of life; stars transformed; stars reborn; dust alive! The dust of the stars is your flesh. The dust of the stars is your blood. Oh, your flesh and blood, full of stars' delight; becomes breath; becomes prayer; dust alive! The dust of the stars is this bread. The dust of the stars is this wine. Oh, this bread and wine, our communion in all things; Flesh of God; dust alive!

Conclude with one minute of contemplative silence.

Earth ~ South ~ Winter ~ Strength

INTERBEING AND INTERCONNECTION

"Wonder is a gateway through which the universe floods in and takes up residence within us." (Brian Swimme and Mary Evelyn Tucker 2011:113)

Resources: A bowl of earth; a glass of water; and a candle.

Song: Melissa Phillipe "There is only one of us" – streaming Apple Music and Spotify.

Begin with three minutes of contemplative silence followed by Acknowledgment of Country. (Push chairs aside and as the song is played you are invited to move slowly, milling around the room and meeting each other giving full eye contact.)

Gather in a circle for the Gaia Meditations (Joanna Macey and John Seed "Thinking like a Mountain – Towards a Council of All Beings" www.rainforestinfo.org.au/deep-eco/TLAM%20text.htm used with permission)

Gaia Meditations

Voice One: What are you? What am I? Intersecting cycles of water, earth, air and fire, that's what I am, that's what you are.

WATER Blood, lymph, mucus, sweat, tears; inner oceans tugged by the moon, tides within and tides without. Streaming fluids floating our cells, washing and nourishing through endless riverways of gut and vein and capillary. Moisture pouring in and through and out of you, of me, in the vast poem of the hydrological cycle. You are that. I am that.

(Glass of water is passed around and each one takes a sip.)

EARTH Matter made from rock and soil. It too is pulled by the moon as the magma circulates through the planet heart and roots suck molecules into biology. Earth pours through us, replacing each cell in the body every seven years. Ashes to ashes, dust to dust, we ingest, incorporate and excrete the earth, are made from earth. I am that. You are that.

(A bowl of earth is passed around and each one touches earth gently.)

AIR The gaseous realm, the atmosphere, the planet's membrane. The inhale and the exhale. Breathing out carbon dioxide to the trees and breathing in their fresh exudations. Oxygen kissing each cell awake, atoms dancing in orderly metabolism, interpenetrating. That dance of the air cycle, breathing the universe in and out again, is what you are, is what I am.

(The Leader invites everyone to take three deep breaths.)

FIRE Fire, from our sun that fuels all life, drawing up plants and raising the waters to the sky to fall again replenishing. The inner furnace of your metabolism burns with the fire of the Big Bang that first sent matter-energy spinning through space and time. And the same fire as the lightning that flashed into the primordial soup catalysing the birth of organic life.

(A candle is lit.)

Voice Two: You were there, I was there, for each cell of our bodies is descended in an unbroken chain from that event. Through the desire of atom for molecule, of molecule for cell, of cell for organism. In our sexuality we can feel ancient stirrings that connect us with plant as well as animal life. We come from them in an unbroken chain — through fish learning to walk the land, feeling scales turning to wings, through the migrations in the ages of ice.

We have been but recently in human form. If Earth's whole history were compressed into twenty-four hours beginning at midnight, organic life would begin only at 3 pm... mammals emerge at 11:30... and from amongst them at only seconds to midnight, our species. (*Pause*)

Voice One: In our long planetary journey we have taken far more ancient forms than these we now wear. Some of these forms we remember in our mother's womb, wear vestigial tails and gills, grow fins for hands. Countless times in that journey we died to old forms, let go of old ways, allowing new ones to emerge. But nothing is ever lost. Though forms pass, all returns. Each worn-out cell consumed, recycled... through mosses, leeches, birds of prey...

Think to your next death. Will your flesh and bones back into the cycle? Surrender. Love the plump worms you will become. Launder your weary being through the fountain of life. (*Pause*)

Voice Two: Beholding you, I behold as well all the different creatures that compose you – the mitochondria in the cells, the intestinal bacteria, the life teeming on the surface of the skin. The great symbiosis that is you. The incredible coordination and cooperation of countless beings. You are that, too, just as your body is part of a much larger symbiosis, living in wider reciprocities. Be conscious of that give-and-take when you move among trees. Breathe your pure carbon dioxide to a leaf and sense it breathing fresh oxygen back to you. Countless times in that journey we died to old forms, let go of old ways, allowing new ones to emerge. But nothing is ever lost. Though forms pass, all returns. (*Pause*)

Voice One: Remember again and again the old cycles of partnership. Draw on them in this time of trouble. By your very nature and the journey you have made, there is in you deep knowledge of belonging. Draw on it now in this time of fear. You have earth-bred wisdom of your interexistence with all that is. Take courage and power in it now, that we may help each other awaken in this time of peril.

Conclude with one minute of contemplative silence.

Earth ~ South ~ Winter ~ Strength

EARTH LAMENT

"Here we can see how precious Earth is as the only living planet that we know, how profoundly it reveals mysteries of the divine, how carefully it should be tended, how great an evil it is to damage its basic life systems, to ruin its beauty and plunder its resources. For these things to be done by Christians or without significant Christian protest is a scandal of the primary order of magnitude." (Thomas Berry 2009:29)

Song: *In the Name of all that is* Jan Novotka streaming Apple Music and Spotify.

This is a group ritual. Prepare and make available two large sheets of paper and textas.

Begin with three minutes of contemplative silence followed by Acknowledgment of Country.

Leader: In the centre of the paper is the word HOPE and you are now invited to write around the word HOPE ways that life systems are being damaged; beauty ruined and resources plundered.

Leader: On another sheet write the words ACTIVE HOPE and write around the words ways that people and groups are working to create a sustainable and healthy planet

Leader: Let us now circle around these words as we sing *In the Name of All that Is*.

In the name of all that is we come together. In the name of the stars and galaxies; in the name of the planets, moons and the sun; in the name of all that is we come.

In the name of all that is we come together. In the name of the ocean and the sea; in the name of the mountain, desert and plain; in the name of all that is we come.

In the name of all that is we come together. In the name of the buffalo and bear; in the name of the turtle, eagle and whale; in the name of all that is we come.

In the name of all that is we come together. In the name of the cactus and the fern; in the name of the flower, tree and the herb; in the name of all that is we come.

In the name of all that is we come together. In the name of the elements of life; in the name of the soil, water and air; in the name of all that is we come.

In the name of all that is we come together. In the name of the children of earth; in the name of the Spirit breathing in all things; in the name of all that is we come.

© 2001 by Jan Novotka's Music, LLC (ASCAP). All rights reserved.

All: In the name of all that is we come together and lament the loss of hope and the ruining of earth's beauty, the plundering of her resources, and the abuse of her life systems. We live in active hope for a healthy future.

Conclude with one minute of contemplative silence.

Earth ~ South ~ Winter ~ Strength

FOREST SUNDAY

"Here we might propose that a viable future for the human community rests largely upon a new relationship between the human communities and the planet on which we dwell. We need to appreciate that both our physical and our spiritual survival depend on the visible world about us. We would have no inner life of mind, imagination or emotion without the wonder, the beauty and the intimacy offered us by the dawn and sunset, the singing birds and the cry of the wolf, by the meadows and all their flowers, by the grandeur of the mountains and the vastness of the sea." (Thomas Berry 2001: *Earthsong Journal*)

(Adapted with permission http://normanhabel.com/)

(*India's Healing Forest Trailer* Nitin Das YouTube link https://youtu.be/9ohmgsh3D7c
Warm up to this ritual by watching this 2 minute trailer.)

Begin with three minutes of contemplative silence followed by Acknowledgment of Country.

Reflect on Psalm 96:12 'All the trees of the forest sing for joy.'

Make an intention to create an opportunity for a forest walk this week.

Leader:	A planet filled with Divine Presence, quivering in the forests, vibrating in the land, pulsating in the wilderness, shimmering in the rivers.
All:	'All the trees of the forest sing for joy.'
Leader:	Mountain ash and eucalypts, quivering ferns and glistening moss!
All:	'All the trees of the forest sing for joy.'
Leader:	Huon pines and ironbark, tall timber where lizards and lichen find their home!
All:	'All the trees of the forest sing for joy.'
Leader:	Green tree frogs and timid moths, ancient owls and swirling bats!
All:	'All the trees of the forest sing for joy.'
Leader:	Forests, on behalf of all humanity, we lament thoughtlessness and greed; destruction and pillaging; death of old growth giants and species breathing their last.
All:	Aware of Great Mystery our hearts stir with pain and loss.

Conclude with one minute of contemplative silence.

Earth ~ South ~ Winter ~ Strength

WHERE YOU ARE STANDING IS HOLY GROUND

"Often we forget that in Genesis, Creation was the very context for our relationship with God. This is something many of us have lost, with much of our lives, work and even worship conducted indoors, shut off from creation. We need to consciously reclaim this, and start with some practical small steps…This needs to be the basis for our action on climate change and sustainability –without a strong inner motivation that comes from our faith, we will be in danger of burnout."
(*Australian Religious Response to Climate Change* (ARRCC: 7)

Begin with three minutes of contemplative silence followed by Acknowledgment of Country. Walk outside to a place where there are many shrubs, plants and leaves. Take this book with you.

Opening Prayer: I see all about me colour, fruits, and signs of life. I give thanks for the gifts I receive daily from these plants. Great Spirit present in all that is I give thanks for the mystery, the creativity and the pulsing of life in all around me. I feel an urgent desire to protect and act for a sustainable future. I make my desire a reality and intend to act from this day forward to be more aware and conscious of my part in creating a climate emergency. Amen.

Reading: "My heart aches as I watch my fellow homo sapiens charging about, conducting 'business as usual' while continuing to increase carbon emissions, knowing full well we are destroying earth as we know it! And since carbon emissions are an inescapable product of our daily lives, I am complicit; we are all complicit." (Mary Southard, used with permission)

Reflective Meditation (Chief Seattle Speech adapted.)

Take a deep breath in and as you breathe out allow your eye to rest on one leaf and say internally "Every part of earth is sacred. I honour you and am in awe."

Take another deep breath in and as you breathe out allow your eye to rest on the sky and say internally "The air is precious, I honour and am in awe of your generosity."

Take another deep breath in and as you breathe out allow your eye to rest on some flowers and say internally "The perfumed flowers are our sisters. I honour you and am in awe."

Litany of Love

Every part of Earth is sacred
I am standing on holy ground

Every shining pine needle, every sandy shore
I am standing on holy ground
Earth is our mother; I am standing on holy ground.

Conclude with one minute of contemplative silence.

Earth ~ South ~ Winter ~ Strength

JESUS TREADS CONSCIOUSLY

"We who have two legs can easily practise meditation. We must not forget to be grateful. We walk for ourselves, and we walk for those who cannot walk. We walk for all living beings – past, present and future." (Thich Nhat Hahn 2006:77)

Begin with three minutes of contemplative silence followed by Acknowledgment of Country. Listen to the song.

Song: *Peace on Earth*, Circle of Friends – streaming on Apple Music and Spotify.

Meditation: Human like Us. (This response by Michael Morwood is used with permission.)

Jesus, human like us you walked consciously in earth.

You walked consciously, human like us.

Jesus, human like us you climbed the mountain to pray.

You walked consciously, human like us.

Jesus, you took time to tread consciously and be mindful.

You walked consciously, human like us.

Jesus, you walked with friends and strangers alike.

You walked consciously, human like us.

Jesus, you spoke to friends whilst on the road to Emmaus.

You walked consciously, human like us.

Jesus, you befriended women, walked with them, and became friends.

You walked consciously, human like us.

Jesus, you taught about justice and peace as you walked by the lake.

You walked consciously, human like us.

To conclude this reflection: A journal idea – Which of the statements touched your own experience most deeply? Which of them felt as if it were calling you home? Conclude when ready in your own time.

Earth ~ South ~ Winter ~ Strength

HOLDING THE GAZE

"We can nurture our capacity for communion by simply living *as if we* are among sentient beings whom we honour and respect. We can do it by cultivating the art of attentive listening, and by respectfully conversing with them as if it is a natural thing to do... As we open ourselves to Earth as a sentient planet, Earth and her beings will respond." (*Earthsong Journal* Wendy Chew 2006:10)

Sit outside in a quiet place where there is foliage, trees and the sound of birds. This meditation invites you to open yourself to the sounds around you. Pay attention to each sound and hold your gaze toward that sound.

Begin with three minutes contemplative silence.

Place your hand on your heart.

Tune into your breath.

Draw upon the source of loving kindness within you, and walk to a nearby tree or bush and place your hand onto the bark. Send loving kindness into this tree. *If you wish you may chant in Gregorian style "Where I'm standing is holy ground; where I'm walking is holy ground; Alleluia, Alleluia, Alleluia."*

This tree makes it possible for you to breathe.

Be grateful and mindful.

Hold your gaze.

Namaste! I see in you nourishing divinity!

Take a few steps and once again pause. Place your hand on your heart.

Tune into your breath.

Draw upon the source of loving kindness within you and gaze up into the sky.

Send loving kindness to all sentient beings that fly.

Be grateful and mindful.

Hold your gaze.

Namaste! I see in you nourishing divinity!

Take another few steps and pause. Draw into yourself the loving kindness of the trees and the birds.

Be grateful and mindful.

Conclude with one minute of contemplative silence.

ELEMENT: AIR

DIRECTION: EAST

SEASON: SPRING

GIFT: TRUTH

Air ~ East ~ Spring ~ Truth

RECONCILIATION

"Kanyini is best expressed in English as the combination of the two words 'responsibility' and 'love', but it is actually a relationship; it is an enormous caring with no limit – it has no timeframe: it is eternal." (David Clark 2014: www.sharingculture.info)

Song: *Kanyini Chant* Bob Randall and Christine Morrison – streaming on Apple Music and Spotify.

Before this ritual, write to participants and ask them to bring an outline of their hand, coloured in and decorated.

Create the *Sea of Hands* in a mandala shape.

Begin with three minutes of contemplative silence followed by Acknowledgment of Country.

Voice One: We are gathering today to raise our consciousness about the importance of recognising that the First Nations People of Australia understand *country* as living and vibrant. "When we talk about traditional 'Country'… we mean something beyond the dictionary definition of the word. For Aboriginal Australians… we might mean homeland, or tribal or clan area and we might mean more than just a place on the map. For us, Country is a word for all the values, places, resources, stories and cultural obligations associated with that area and its features. It describes the entirety of our ancestral domains. While they may all no longer necessarily be the title-holders to land, Aboriginal and Torres Strait Islander Australians are still connected to the Country of their ancestors and most consider themselves the custodians or caretakers of their land." (Mick Dodson 2009)

(All circle around the *Sea of Hands* and move around slowly whilst listening to the Kanyini Chant [9 minutes]).

(Sit in a circle with the *Sea of Hands* in the centre.)

All: There can be no reconciliation without justice. There can be no justice without understanding. There can be no understanding without standing in the shoes of another and there can be no standing without being still. (Author Unknown)

Voice Two: We remember and acknowledge the original inhabitants of Australia, both past and present, and lament that their land was taken away from them and no treaty was made.

All: We lament.

Voice Three: We remember the families who suffered trauma, loss and grief when their children were removed.

All: We lament.

Voice One: We remember the massacres.

All: We lament.

Conclude with one minute of contemplative silence.

Air ~ East ~ Spring ~ Truth

CREATIVE INTENTIONING

"**We must embrace a universal communion; how we treat creation is how we treat each other. I say it again: everything is interconnected and we are on a wonderful pilgrimage bonded with other creatures…**" (LS: 92)

A bowl is placed in the centre of the room and people sit in a circle and each one has five sticky notes and a pen. A candle is lit next to the empty bowl.

Begin with three minutes of contemplative silence followed by Acknowledgment of Country.

Presider: Please think of your intention, a person you want to remember and pray for today. Write their name and place in the bowl.

The bowl is passed around the circle.

Presider: Please think of a country "where some people live in degrading poverty" (LS: 90) and write the name and place in the bowl.

The bowl is passed around the circle.

Presider: Please now think of an animal that you know is already extinct or close to extinction and write the name and place in the bowl.

The bowl is passed around the circle.

Presider: Please now think of an animal that is an endangered species and write the name and place in the bowl.

The bowl is passed around the circle.

Presider: Please now take a moment to reflect on the words of Pope Francis – "If humanity loses its orientation to goodness and beauty, if we lose sight of what brings us together as a human family, then no technical solution to the ecology crisis can succeed. We people of faith must live convincingly ourselves, embracing justice, peace, simpler and sustainable living, and solidarity with the poor. If we are violators of nature ourselves, then we must correct out own behaviors first." (LS: 200)

Pause for reflection.

All: Awake to Divine Presence in our midst, we entrust our intention to the healing energy of the universe. In the meanwhile, we intend to act in trust that all things work together for our good and the good of all – human and non-human.

Conclude with one minute of contemplative silence.

Air ~ East ~ Spring ~ Truth

BREATH

"… much of the writing in this book is poetry. As poetry releases one from many constraints of the cerebral, logic processes of essays, and allows what I would call Spirit to be glimpsed."(Trevor Parton, 2017:11)

Song: *By Breath* Sarah Thomsen – streaming on Apple Music and Spotify.

Begin with three minutes of contemplative silence followed by Acknowledgment of Country.

This ritual can be prayed outside.

Leader: Today we will adapt *Lectio Divina* to reflect on this poem by Trevor Parton (used with permission) and as we gather in this circle let us listen to a reading of the poem.

"*Lectio Divina…* is an ancient practice and can include any sacred text – a passage that moves you, a poem you love, or an image that is calling for your attention." (Christine Valters Paintner, 2011:18)

BREATH

    Hurry pilgrim to the land of slowness
    Where each breath becomes precious
    And more precious yet as time passes.
    The air of millennia holds us in embrace
    Where falling spiralling feather spans eternity,
    And swallow swoops in
    To gather its softness for her nest.
    And the eagle spirals lazily ever higher
    On hidden currents of the same shared air.
    Space needs time, for the time being.
    Time fills space like a cup of tea.
    We breathe time, until time stands still.
    When time stands still for us
    We step outside space
    And stop becoming,
    Because we have come home
    Where life transcends even self itself.
    Where a new symphony commences every instant;

Air ~ East ~ Spring ~ Truth

The conductor reading the music we have left.

Leader: Let us listen to the poem being read again and this time you will be invited to share one word that stays with you.

Circle sharing with pauses to allow slowing down, becoming fully present, and maintaining a sense of awe and wonder as each one speaks.

Leader: Let us listen to the poem for a third time and you are asked to listen for an invitation that stays with you.

Circle sharing with pauses to allow slowing down, becoming fully present, and maintaining a sense of awe and wonder as each one speaks.

Group Sharing: In groups of three share favourite images and metaphors from this poem and what you are being invited to allow emergence in your own life.

Return to the large circle for A Breath Meditation.

Alternate Nostril Breathing

Leader: Come to quiet and close your eyes.
Gently rest your index and middle finger of your right hand on your forehead.
Close your right nostril with your thumb.
Inhale slowly and soundlessly through your left nostril.
Close your left nostril with your ring finger and simultaneously open your right nostril by removing your thumb.
Exhale slowly and soundlessly and as thoroughly as possible through your right nostril.
Inhale through your right nostril.
Close your right nostril with your thumb and open your left nostril.
Exhale through your left nostril.
Leave your index and middle finger of your right hand on your forehead.
(Leader repeats these directions 5-6 times) Come to a natural ending.

Listen to the Song - *By Breath*

Conclude with one minute of contemplative silence.

Air ~ East ~ Spring ~ Truth

ATMOSPHERE SUNDAY

"We remember the atmosphere, the breath of God that gives us life, the oxygen emerging from forest leaves and deep ocean plankton, the winds that bring us weather and the breezes that stir our senses. We remember and rejoice." (Norm Habel)

(Adapted with permission www. normanhabel.com/) Gather gum leaves for this ritual.

Song: *Within All* by Jan Novotka streaming on Apple Music and Spotify.

Begin with three minutes of contemplative silence followed by Acknowledgment of Country.

Leader: As we stand outside in the atmosphere, we give thanks for the daily gifts we receive. We become mindful of every layer of moisture and air, from ground level to the ozone heights.

Take a deep breath; inhale the atmosphere, the Spirit of God.

All: **We give thanks for breeze and wind.**

Leader: Lift your faces to the breeze and be mindful of wild winds that stir the seas, and soft breezes that carry the pollen.

All: **We give thanks for breeze and wind**

Leader: We now take the eucalyptus leaves in our hands so that we may connect with our non-human relatives.

Leader: Take the eucalyptus leaves in your hands and rub them together. Take a deep breath and inhale the aroma. Take another deep breath to recall times when you experienced the thin air high on a mountain, the salt air at the seaside or the moist air in a fog.

All: **We lament as we hold these fragrant leaves that we have filled the atmosphere with pollutants, toxins, fumes and carbon dioxide, creating a greenhouse in the air above us, with a global warming that changes weather and upsets the current balance of nature.**

Song: Within All

We all share the same Breath and Essence.

Within all is Infinite Being.

Within all, within all, within all that is.

We all share in One Life and Presence.

Deep within all is Spirit's light.

Within all, within all, within all that is.

Within all, within all, within all that is.

© *2006 by Jan Novotka's Music, LLC (ASCAP). All rights reserved.*

Conclude with one minute of contemplative silence.

Air ~ East ~ Spring ~ Truth

JESUS IN THE FRESH AIR

"**Jesus 'saves' us by 'setting us free from ideas and images suggesting that God is distant from our everyday living." (Michael Morwood, 2018:59)**

Begin with three minutes of contemplative silence followed by Acknowledgment of Country.

Song: *Like a Feather on the Breath of God* by Susan Lincoln & Craig Toungate – streaming on Apple Music and Spotify. Listen to this song and sit in a solitary place outside and reflect on these words, praying them slowly and mindfully.

Meditation: Human like Us. (This response by Michael Morwood is used with permission.)

Jesus, human like us you walked and walked in the fresh air.

You breathed in air and breathed it out, human like us.

Jesus, human like us you sat under trees and listened for the sounds of the breeze.

You breathed in air and breathed it out, human like us.

Jesus, you took time to go into the mountains and be grateful.

You breathed in air and breathed it out, human like us.

Jesus, you ate with friends and strangers alike.

You breathed in air and breathed it out, human like us.

Jesus, you are way, truth and life.

You breathed in air and breathed it out, human like us.

Jesus, you befriended women and men and treated all fairly.

You breathed in air and breathed it out, human like us.

Jesus, you revealed the Spirit of Life.

You breathed in air and breathed it out, human like us.

To conclude this reflection: A journal idea – Which of the statements touched your own experience most deeply? Which of them felt as if it were calling you home? Conclude when ready in your own time.

Air ~ East ~ Spring ~ Truth

A GROUP SPRING RITUAL: THE LILAC TREE

"In many latitudes, forests drop leaves in the fall and leaf out in the spring, and we take this cycle for granted. But if we take a closer look, the whole thing is a big mystery, because it means that trees need something very important: a sense of time." (Peter Wohlleben: 2016:147)

Group Warm-Up: Gather inside and watch together a one minute YouTube of Lilac growing in spring. https://youtu.be/HIDIKD6eknc

Begin with three minutes of contemplative silence followed by Acknowledgment of Country. Gather in a circle outside. In the centre of the circle are bunches of lilac and a plate of spring fruit including apples, bananas, berries, mangoes, oranges and pineapples.

Leader: Let us go around the circle and start by saying 'I am… and today I bring to the circle Memories of Spring.

A second circle share answers the question "What do I love the most about lilac?"

Leader: "Australian creatures associated with spring are eagle, rooster, seagull, spider and owl and the colours of spring here are pink, lilac and rose." (Dr Tricia Szirom 2011:64)

Leader: We will now adapt *Lectio Divina* to reflect on a poem by Brenda Peddigrew rsm. (Used with permission https://soulwinds.ca/brenda.html)

"*Lectio Divina*…is an ancient practice and can include any sacred text – a passage that moves you, a poem you love, or an image that is calling for your attention." (Christine Valters Paintner 2011:18)

Leader: As we gather in this circle, let us listen to a first reading of the poem.

The Lilac Tree

When that first hard bud emerged
on the lilac tree next to the back door
I almost wondered where it came from.
The icy winter, long and hard and lasting, lasting,
Seemed to seal the ground and decimate
any opening for the slightest shoot.
But there it was, facing me
at eye level, inescapable.
Clinging as it seemed to be,
winter's chains were broken.

How could it not be also with me?
I thought. How could it not be
that the hardness of my own heart -
eclipsing any possibility of a soft soul -
could also send forth a bud, a shoot,

Air ~ East ~ Spring ~ Truth

from a place I thought
long dead or didn't even know about?

Nothing ever ends.
Nothing. Ever. Ends.
Or is finished. The green is witness
and wonder, the outward sign
of life infinite and not yet imagined.
And isn't that sacrament?
The outward sign of inward grace?

Well, grace is nothing but a slight shift,
a lifting of a weight I didn't even know
was there. But relieved at its going,
oh inestimably, ecstatically relieved.

Not much different, really
from the downy new bud on this lilac tree
or the fuzzy leaf bursting out now
everywhere I look.
And I among them, one other sacrament
emerging from the frozen season.

Winter will be back, no doubt about that.
But with every exhilarating spring
life gets larger
without and within
like the reaching lilac tree standing sentinel at the back door.

Leader: Let us listen to the poem being read again and this time you will be invited to share one word that stays with you.

Circle sharing with pauses to allow slowing down, becoming fully present, and maintaining a sense of awe and wonder as each one speaks.

Leader: Let us listen to the poem for a third time and you are asked to listen for an invitation that stays with you.

Circle sharing with pauses to allow slowing down, becoming fully present, and maintaining a sense of awe and wonder as each one speaks.

Group Sharing: In groups of three, share favourite images and metaphors from this poem and what you are being invited to allow emergence in your own life.

Return to the large circle and conclude with one minute of contemplative silence and then celebrate by sharing the plate of spring fruit together.

Air ~ East ~ Spring ~ Truth

A SPRING CONTEMPLATIVE POEM

"Trees are the lungs of Earth, maintaining the balance of nature as their seasonal changes create a habitat for plants and wild life. They are nature's way of renewing the air that we breathe: they absorb carbon dioxide and give oxygen, which enables all living beings to breathe." (Nellie McLaughlin 2004:187)

Begin with three minutes of contemplative silence followed by Acknowledgment of Country.

(Used with permission Carmel Crameri RSJ – the poem was written whilst studying at Genesis Farm in the USA.)

Mindfully walk to an outside space where there are many trees and take a copy of this poem with you. After reading the poem a couple of times close your eyes and listen to the sounds of nature around you. Allow the words of the poem to fall into you like a waterfall.

Tree
    O Tree of ancient beauty
    Whose branches hold the birth of breath
    Wherein the sun filters in royal fashion
    And lights up the leaves in shimmering nobility
    Reminder of the Universe song
    Whose music is conveyed in the murmur of the wind
    As she plays her notes of delicate touch
    On the green foliage
    I marvel as I gaze upon you
    Whose praise of the divine creative energy
    Emerges in the task of being
    Simply being
    You teach me
    You touch me
    You life me
    As you stand in your magnificent gown of being Tree.

Conclude your mindfulness meditation with one minute of contemplative silence.

Air ~ East ~ Spring ~ Truth

A MINDFULNESS WALK

"Everybody needs beauty as well as bread, places to play in and pray in where nature may heal and give strength to body and soul alike." (John Muir 1912 *The Yosemite*, reprinted 2007)

Begin with three minutes of contemplative silence followed by Acknowledgment of Country. The Presider will walk with your group, inviting you to pause for reflection. If this is a solitary walk, please take this book with you and lead yourself.

Presider: Walk now for five minutes mindfully and as you walk watch your step, slow your pace, feel the breath of the air, notice any colour, look up to the sky and be aware of plants, shrubs, trees. Pause and soak in the beauty. Tread consciously. Stop from time to time and touch one of the plants, internally acknowledging Great Mystery present in you and in them.

Presider: Pause now and take a few deep breaths.

Very mindfully and slowly, walk the following mantras one by one.

Presider: "I am walking mindfully."

Presider: "Treading consciously in earth."

Presider: "I am part of all that is."

Presider: "Watching out for signs of growth."

Presider: "Heeding all the sounds around."

Presider: Walk now for another five minutes mindfully and as you walk watch your step, slow your pace, feel the breath of the air, notice any colour, look up to the sky and be aware of plants, shrubs, trees. Pause and soak in the beauty. Tread consciously. Stop from time to time and touch one of the plants, internally acknowledging Great Mystery present in you and in them

Presider: "I am walking mindfully."

Presider: "Treading consciously on earth."

Presider: "I am part of all that is."

Presider: "Watching out for signs of growth."

Presider: "Heeding all the sounds around."

Presider: Walk now for a final five minutes and give thanks for all that you see, hear and touch. Tread consciously and with reverence.

Conclude with one minute of contemplative silence.

Air ~ East ~ Spring ~ Truth

REVERENCING ALL LIFE: A MORNING WALK

"A first step to live harmoniously within creation is to reverence the marvellous diversity of life forms." (Kevin Treston 2003:14)

This is a meditative praying of Psalm 104 (adapted) and is best done outside walking. You will need a copy of this book. The mantras below are each best walked to seven steps.

"Walking in the morning light; treading consciously in earth; greeting morning with delight."

Begin with three minutes of contemplative silence followed by Acknowledgment of Country.

Then read verse one of the psalm.

The heavens stretch out like a tent; radiance covers the waters; the clouds ride on the wings of the wind; fire refines our deepest thoughts.

Continue walking: "Walking in the morning light; treading consciously in earth; greeting morning with delight."

Pause under a tree or near some water and read the next verse of the psalm.

The earth is set strong and secure; many waters become rivers and lakes and mighty oceans; mountains rise; valleys become low; life springs abundantly.

Continue walking: "Walking in the morning light; treading consciously in earth; greeting morning with delight."

Pause where you can hear the morning sounds and read the next verse of the psalm.

Springs flow into the valleys; giving drink to all life forms; with the air the birds inhabit the trees and sing among the branches; the sounds of creation stir the morning air.

Continue walking: "Walking in the morning light; treading consciously in earth; greeting morning with delight."

Pause and sit under a tree and listen to the morning sounds. Take a few breaths of fresh air and become mindful of the next verse of the psalm.

Love brings forth all that is evolving; grass for the cattle; plants to be cultivated; fruit of the vine that gives us wine; oil and healing herbs; bread sustains us; trees are watered abundantly and the sun and moon gift us with the air we breathe; every living creature, life form has its home: the birds nest in the trees; the goats up in the mountains; rocks provide protection as creatures roam earth; in wisdom all is created.

Continue walking: "Walking in the morning light; treading consciously in earth; greeting morning with delight."

Conclude with one minute of contemplative silence.

Air ~ East ~ Spring ~ Truth

COMMUNITY EARTH RITUAL: SPRING EQUINOX

"Spring returns, again. The Spirits of Renewal and Rebirth wake up. In the beginning is the awakening… the changing light… returning birds… warm breezes… budding trees… breathing, stretching, pushing, grunting and struggling to come to life." (Diann L. Neu 2002:53)

This is a link to Glenys Livingstone's website and there you can purchase the spring meditation https://pagaian.org/pagaian-prayers-invoking-her/

A Possible Process for Creating a Ritual – Remote Preparation

For several year, a community group has been meeting to celebrate the Spring Equinox and create a ritual together.

Two weeks before the scheduled ritual, an email is sent to the group to remind them to reflect on autumn and allow their contemplative stance to flow freely.

"For those of you who are coming for the first time we have been working with the idea of a 'contemplative stance' – allowing anything that emerges in us as spring nears – thought; idea; action; musing; daydreaming; synchronicity, etc. to make a note and bring something to celebrate this at the spring equinox ritual.

"We will celebrate with whatever you bring to contribute to the ritual – out of your reflections since the last ritual – poetry; music; sacred space décor; symbols; readings; movement; drama, dance; and art works."

Suggested Process for Creating a Ritual on the Day

Gather in a circle and acknowledge the land and original inhabitants of country.

Begin with three minutes of contemplative silence.

The leader invites each person one by one to share what they have bought to the ritual.

The listening process is discerning and appreciative.

Using contemplative listening (one person speaks at a time and whatever is suggested is accepted without interruption or disagreement), the group then suggests possible placing and timing of the texts, décor, music, dance, etc. This usually works out smoothly and with great respect for the gifts shared among the group.

The ritual is enacted.

Conclude with one minute of contemplative silence.

Air ~ East ~ Spring ~ Truth

SPIRIT PRESENT IN ALL THAT IS

"Everything born out of that creation – including humans – mirrors the divine presence, and especially its potential for cocreativity. Energy is the primary stuff through which the Spirit operates." (Diarmuid O'Murchu 2017:46)

Begin with three minutes of contemplative silence followed by Acknowledgment of Country. This is designed as a group ritual.

A candle is lit in the circle and two voices will read the reflections written by Diarmuid O'Murchu.

Voice One: "God's presence with us, and the divine incarnational insertion among us, *belongs, first and foremost, to creation itself.*" (ibid: 48)

Minute of Silence timed with the Tibetan Bell. (An option is to download a free app entitled *Centring Prayer* which has bell tones.)

All: In me now in love and grace; Divine Spirit in the world; calling me to love anew and break fresh ground generously.

Voice Two: **11 billion years ago:** The seventh chakra, marking the gift of LIGHT! We celebrate the resilience of the creative Spirit weaving creation through the paradox of light and darkness, illuminating the mystery through which all creation thrives, enlightening our understanding of how creation works, and brightening our future with hope and purpose. (http://www.diarmuid13.com/) (Used with permission.)

Voice One: 'In First Nation's spirituality, the Great Spirit denotes God's involvement in the entire creation; particularly over the several billennia before planet earth came to be." (ibid: 48)

Minute of Silence timed with the Tibetan Bell.

All: In me now in love and grace; Divine Spirit in the world; calling me to love anew and break fresh ground generously.

Voice Two: **10 billion years ago:** The sixth chakra, marking the gift of WISDOM! We celebrate the wisdom and intelligence which is innate to creation at every level of its unfolding story, the well-spring which endows everything in creation to act wisely for the good of the whole, and the source from which human intelligence also emanates. (http://www.diarmuid13.com/) (Used with permission.)

Voice One: "In a word, the human body is intimately linked not merely with earth body but with the cosmic body as well. Incarnationally, our corporal identity is that of sun-energy, stardust, and the interwoven complexity of several energy forces belonging to the vast womb of our evolving universe." (ibid: 49)

Minute of Silence timed with the Tibetan Bell.

All: In me now in love and grace; Divine Spirit in the world; calling me to love

	anew and break fresh ground generously.
Voice Two:	**9 billion years ago:** The fifth chakra, marking the gift of COMMUNICATION. We celebrate creation's potential to relate and communicate, to articulate the richness of its life and meaning – in a narrative imbued with complexity and wonder. Our human capacity for speech and word belong to creation's innate potential to communicate and articulate meaning. (http://www.diarmuid13.com/) (Used with permission.)
Voice One:	"Long before religion ever unfolded in the formal ways we know today, our ancient ancestors engaged with Holy Mystery and appropriated its benevolence through a range of rituals and ensuing ethical behaviours." (ibid: 50)

Minute of Silence timed with the Tibetan Bell.

All:	In me now in love and grace; Divine Spirit in the world; calling me to love anew and break fresh ground generously.
Voice Two:	**8 billion years ago:** The fourth chakra, celebrating IMMUNITY and the capacity for right relating. We celebrate creation's capacity for healthy and wholesome living, facilitated through mutually enriching relationships with the diverse creatures that constitute the canopy of universal life. (http://www.diarmuid13.com/) (Used with permission.)
Voice One:	"We are an interdependent species whose growth, development, and evolution are integrally connected with the surrounding web of life." (ibid: 55)
All:	In me now in love and grace; Divine Spirit in the world; calling me to love anew and break fresh ground generously.
Voice Two:	**7 billion years ago**: The third chakra, marking the invitation to mutual EMPOWERMENT. We celebrate the mutuality through which interdependence thrives, empowering every aspect of creation towards the realisation of its true potential, liberating freedom and hope for future possibility (http://www.diarmuid13.com/) (Used with permission.)
Voice One:	**6 billion years ago:** The second chakra, marking GENERATIVITY and erotic birthing. In a creation of prodigious fertility we celebrate the fruitfulness and creative abundance we see around us, and we give thanks for the pleasures and joys of sexual intimacy. (http://www.diarmuid13.com/) (Used with permission)
Voice Two:	**5 billion years ago:** The base chakra, GROUNDING our presence in earth and in the body. At every level of creation, energy begets form, and all form assumes embodied presence. The cosmos, the galaxies, the earth, landscapes, persons, and bacteria are all embodied expressions through which the presence of living Spirit becomes grounded in creation.

Conclude ritual with one minute of contemplative silence.

Air ~ East ~ Spring ~ Truth

EXAMEN OF CONSCIOUSNESS

"Our insistence that each human being is an image of God should not make us overlook the fact that each creature has its own purpose. None is superfluous. The entire material universe speaks of God's love and boundless affection for us. Soil, water, mountains: everything is, as it were, a caress of God." (LS: 84)

This is a reflective *Examen of Consciousness* based on findings taken from **the Mercy International Reflection Process.***

"Threaded throughout the visions and the actions were references to the need for a new theology, new images of God, a new language and new conversations." (Mercy International Reflection Process Review 2017:12)

Begin with three minutes of contemplative silence followed by Acknowledgment of Country.

Sit outside in a quiet place with a copy of this book for your reflection.

Examen of Consciousness: New Language

Am I willing to write my own Beatitudes for today?

Am I willing to prepare the Stations of the Cross using the story and experience of a girl who was trafficked?

Am I willing to write my own laments about the displacement of persons for use in prayer and in liturgy in the style of biblical psalms?

Am I willing to continue to read and think about creation theology despite the differences in understanding among us?

Am I willing to organise a Holy Hour each Wednesday evening for 'immediate' world attention – wars/ catastrophe/devastation/refugees/hunger/floods, etc.?

Am I willing to use a creation-centred Ritual for Evening Prayer?

Mindfulness Meditation: Look around at the non-human life around you; experience the breeze; look up into the sky and breathe in and out several times to allow the questions to flow through you.

Examen of Consciousness: New Understandings

Am I willing to dialogue with Celtic, Indigenous and Indigenous Australian understandings and practices in relationship to Earth, self and other?

Am I willing to live in the present moment/be present to the presence of the other?

Am I willing to speak with homeless people I see on the streets? Am I willing to face my fears, judgmental attitudes and assumptions?

Air ~ East ~ Spring ~ Truth

Mindfulness Meditation: For a second time, look around at the non-human life around you; experience the breeze; look up into the sky and breathe in and out several times to allow the questions to flow through you.

Possible actions responding to "The Cry of Earth"

(You are invited to a quiet reflection on these suggestions, choosing one that you can work with immediately.)

Calls to Transformation

Examine my complicity in consumerism through continuing reflection and a mantra "may I live gratefully and simply today".

Examine my willingness to develop policies and strategies that facilitate public action, e.g. refugees, climate change, sustainable living.

Examine my awareness/connection/participation with Earth and each other by acting out of the eighth spiritual and corporal work of Mercy: show mercy to our common home.

Examine my willingness to connect with other groups around sustainable living (e.g., local government organisations, similar groups locally and globally in my town or city).

Examine my willingness to encourage ethical investments linked with impacts of climate change.

Examine my willingness to keep myself informed and support groups such as Campaign for Nuclear Disarmament and Friends of the Earth.

Examine my willingness to celebrate creation and care for creation in our parish liturgies, using topics relating to the care for our environment in Lenten Groups, Social Justice Sundays and homilies.

Examine my willingness to add Pope Francis' two new Corporal and Spiritual Works of Mercy (Care for our Common Home and Grateful Contemplation of Earth) into my regular contemplative practice?

Examine my willingness to network with groups addressing climate change in my town or city?

Mindfulness Meditation: For a third time, look around at the non-human life around you; experience the breeze; look up into the sky and breathe in and out several times to allow the questions to flow through you.

Conclude with one minute of silent contemplation.

*From the *Mercy International Reflection Process Guide Book*. Editor, Adele Howard rsm. © 2018.

Air ~ East ~ Spring ~ Truth

MANTRAS: A SPRINGTIME MEDITATON

"… begin creating prayers and liturgies that support this new engagement and new spirituality and new ethics with creation." (Sean McDonagh 2016)

Choose an outdoor setting for this contemplative ritual.

Song: *Earth Community* Jan Novotka -streaming on Apple Music and Spotify.

Begin with three minutes of contemplative silence followed by Acknowledgment of Country

Stand and Face the East: Today I welcome the Season of Spring. I face the East and draw in a deep breath of fresh air. I invoke a blessing on this time of silent reflection.

Close your eyes: Breathe in the sounds of Earth Community.

Open your eyes: Breathe out the sounds of spring.

Close your eyes: Breathe in the smells of Earth Community.

Open your eyes: Breathe out the smells of spring.

Close your eyes: Breathe in the sights of Earth Community.

Open your eyes: Breathe out the sight of spring.

Close your eyes: Breathe in the taste of Earth Community.

Open your eyes: Breathe out the taste of spring.

Close your eyes: Breathe in and allow yourself to be touched by Earth Community.

Open your eyes: Breathe out and feel the touch of spring.

Mindfulness Meditation: read; pause; and savour…

Compassionately I choose
To sit reverently in earth.
In this inner stillness now
Evolving and Unfolding.
Consciously, I reverently
Appreciate all that is now
Binding me to one and All!

(Listen to *Earth Community*) Reverently, Consciously, Compassionately; I want to walk; I want to live within the earth Community© *1995 by Jan Novotka's Music, LLC (ASCAP). All rights reserved.*

Final blessing: *May you be blessed from above by a dove, from below by a swallow, but now and then by a blue wren! (Norm Habel)*

Conclude with one minute of contemplative silence.

Air ~ East ~ Spring ~ Truth

STARGAZING IN SPRING

"The debris of dying stars has enriched the mixture of gases from which new stars, planets and people are born. We are the grandchildren of supernovae. We are indeed made from stardust." (Denis Edwards 1992:41)

Group Ritual: Gather inside to watch together a YouTube of the 2018 Vatican Observatory Summer School. (https://youtu.be/0_-VIf38Cg4)

Begin with three minutes of contemplative silence followed by Acknowledgment of Country.

Small groups of three: What surprised me about this video?

Gather in large group for *contemplative listening* to the following question:

"What does being made from stardust mean for me?"

Contemplative Listening requires attentive, mindful hearing of the words being shared by each person speaking one at a time, and not interrupting or arguing – simply accepting each person's perspective.

Choose a place outside at night time and, using a yoga mat or something similar, lie down so that you can observe, contemplate and reflect on the night sky.

One person with a torch silently reads these phrases:

As you look up at the night sky become aware of your breathing. Note the rhythm of your breathing. Feel the night air coming through your nostrils and filling your lungs, expanding in your chest and abdomen, and then release, let go and prepare for another deep breath.

Breathe in the stars and planets and breathe out wonder.

Breathe in the darkness of the night and breathe out gratitude.

Breathe in the silence of the evening and breathe out peace.

Breathe in and breathe out several times.

Place your hand over your heart and say in your mind's eye "I am filled with loving kindness", "I am peaceful and at ease", "I am well", "I am happy".

Bring to mind people and beings all over the world and in your mind's eye say "You are filled with loving kindness". "You are peaceful and at ease". "You are well". "You are happy".

Breathe in the stars and planets and breathe out thanks.

Conclude with one minute of silent contemplation.

Air ~ East ~ Spring ~ Truth

SKY SUNDAY REFLECTION

"**You are the dark that holds the stars in intimate distance that spun the whirling, whirling world into existence; let's meet at the confluence where you flow into me and one breath swirls between our lungs.**" (Drew Dellinger 2011:33)

(Adapted with permission www. normanhabel.com/)

Sky refers to the all the domains of creation above and around Earth. Sky especially refers to the domains close to Earth – the wind, the clouds, the air – the atmosphere.

It is appropriate to create a sense of sky in your prayer space with various symbols of domains around Earth – stars, galaxies, clouds. Images of sunrise, moonlight and storms can be projected on screens.

Begin with three minutes of contemplative silence followed by Acknowledgment of Country.

Presider: We celebrate this Sunday with the skies. We celebrate with the clouds, the winds, the dusk and the dawn. We listen to the sounds of sky proclaiming Divine Presence. We stand in awe before the vast reaches of space above us and give thanks for the fragile piece of stardust we call Earth.

Response: Holy! Holy! Holy! Sky canopy of light. Holy! Holy! Holy!

Presider: We give thanks!
Blessed be the subtle orange skies at dawn and the bold red skies at sunset.

Response: We give thanks!
Blessed be the sky proclaiming across the globe, reminding us of sacred presence with the evening stars.

Response: We give thanks!
Blessed be the air, the moisture, the oxygen, and the wind.

Response: We give thanks!
Blessed be the life-giving drops of rain, that gives hope and healing to Earth.

Response: We give thanks!

(Here those gathered may like to share a story of the night sky; camping; or stargazing; or watching the sky light up with stars after sunset.)

Blessing: May we continue to be awake to the billions of years since planet earth was formed and be grateful for our common home.

Conclude with one minute of contemplative silence.

Air ~ East ~ Spring ~ Truth

AN ANCIENT PRAYER

"The future attracts and invites us to move forward, informing every aspect of our being and becoming. We strive for something more because deep in our hearts the Spirit lures us to do so. The restlessness within us is a divine one, the fruit of the enlivening, energising and empowering Spirit, the same Spirit that blows where it wills and never ceases to amaze and surprise us." (Diarmuid O'Murchu, 2012: 83)

(Used with permission Diarmuid O'Murchu http://www.diarmuid13.com/special-prayers)

(Based on John Dominic Crossan (2010), *The Greatest Prayer*) "*We are as human beings co-responsible with the Householder for the household of the world.*" (p. 50)

Begin with three minutes of contemplative silence followed by Acknowledgment of Country.
Pray:

>O Cosmic Householder,
>Source of our wisdom, protector and provider,
>embracing all that dwells in the Heavens,
>naming all for holiness and justice,
>in the Companionship of Empowerment,
>spread throughout the entire creation,
>as willed by Holy Wisdom.
>In justice, may all be sustained by daily food,
>and relieved of the burden of crippling debts.
>Lead us not into collusion with any type of violence,
>and deliver us from all forms of violent oppression.
>For yours is the empowering desire to radiate on earth
>the non-violent justice of enduring hope. Amen.

Reflective Song: *Aramaic Lord's Prayer* Susan Lincoln & Craig Toungate – streaming on Apple Music and Spotify.

Slowly savour and pray this special prayer:

>O Cosmic Birther of all radiance and vibration! Soften the ground of our being
>and carve out a space within us where your presence can abide.
>Fill us with your creativity so that we may be empowered to bear
>the fruit of your mission.
>Let each of our actions bear fruit in accordance with your desire.
>Endow us with the wisdom to produce and share what each being needs
>to grow and flourish. Untie the tangled threads of destiny that bind us,
>as we release others from the entanglement of past mistakes.
>Do not let us be seduced by that which would divert us from our true purpose,
>but illuminate the opportunities of the present moment.
>For you are the ground and fruitful vision, the birth, power and fulfilment
>as all is gathered and made whole once again.
>
>(Based on the original Aramaic – Neil Douglas Klotz)

Conclude with one minute of contemplative silence.

Air ~ East ~ Spring ~ Truth

THE BEATITUDES AS INSPIRED BY THE ORIGINAL ARAMAIC

"Companionship of empowerment… provides a blistering critique of all power seeking, conjuring an alternative option for power sharing, and the empowerment of all who have been disenfranchised by manipulation and exploitation." (Diarmuid O'Murchu 2017: 188)

(Used with permission Diarmuid O'Murchu http://www.diarmuid13.com/special-prayers)

(Gather in a circle in the evening with 8 tea light candles burning in the centre.)

Begin with three minutes of contemplative silence followed by Acknowledgment of Country.

Voice One: Fulfilled are those who devote themselves to the link of Spirit; the design of the universe is rendered through them. **All:** Fulfilled are those…

Voice Two: Healed are those who weep for their frustrated desire; they shall see the face of fulfilment in a new form. **All:** Healed are those…

Voice Three: Healthy are they who have softened what is rigid within; they shall be open to receive the splendour of earth's fruits. **All:** Healthy are they…

Voice Four: Happy are they who long deeply for a world of right relationships, they shall be encircled by the birth of a new society. **All:** Happy are they…

Voice One: Healthy are they who from the inner womb birth forth compassion; they shall feel its warm arms embracing them. **All:** Healthy are they…

Voice Two: Happy are they whose passion radiates with deep abiding purpose; they shall envision the furthest extent of life's wealth. **All:** Happy are they…

Voice Three: Healed are those who bear the fruit of sympathy and safety for all; they shall hasten the coming of God's new creation. **All:** Healed are those…

Voice Four: Healing to those who have been shattered within – from seeking wholesome rest; theirs is the ruling principle of the Cosmos. **All:** Healing to those…

Voice One: Blessed are you when you are reproached and driven away by the clamour of evil on all sides, for my sake. Know deep joy even in your loss for this is the secret for claiming your expanded home in the universe; it is a sign of the prophets and prophetesses to feel the disunity around them intensely.

(Based on Neil Douglas-Klotz, *Prayers of the Cosmos* 1990:44-76)

(Turn off the lights and sit in a circle with the candles burning.)

Conclude with one minute of contemplative silence.

Air ~ East ~ Spring ~ Truth

LAUDATO SI': AIR

"We have forgotten that we ourselves are the dust of earth; our very bodies are made up of her elements, we breathe her air and we receive life and refreshment from her waters." (LS: 2)

(Gather outside and sit in a circle. Light incense sticks in the centre of the circle. One person leads the guided meditation. That person will have a copy and everyone else will sit with their eyes closed.)

Begin with three minutes of contemplative silence followed by Acknowledgment of Country.

Leader: Settle into a quiet place within yourself. Close your eyes and take some deep breaths and become still within yourself.

Allow any thoughts or distractions to come and go. It is helpful if they come to say the word *thinking*. See them as clouds passing over. (*Pause*)

Gradually become conscious of your body, do a whole body scan from your toes, ankles, legs, knees, lower bodies, upper bodies, neck, face, arms, fingers, head to include your whole torso. (*Pause*)

Relax and rest in the knowledge that your body is open and alert. (*Pause*)

Become aware of your feelings. Note any tension or anxiety and allow it to float away. (*Pause*)

Imagine yourself sinking down into a beautiful garden space that is below the mountain upon which you are standing. You drop down slowly by taking the rocky steps that are cut into the side of the mountain (10, 9, 8, 7, 6, 5, 4, 3, 2, 1) and stop and look around at the beautiful garden before you.

Imagine yourself walking into the garden. (*Pause*)

Smell the plants and trees. (*Pause*) Stop and look at the colours. (*Pause*)…

Take a seat in the garden and listen. (*Pause*) Take in some deep breaths of air.

Listen to the ancient depths, your ancestors and all that has gone before you… (*Pause*) In this SACRED NOW hear Pope Francis saying "Each year sees the disappearance of thousands of plant and animal species which we will never know, which our children will never see, because they have been lost forever" (LS: 33).

Continue sitting in the garden and listen to your heart and mind. What is your response? (*Pause*)

Keeping your eyes closed, begin walking back to the steps cut into the side of the mountain and begin the ascent (1, 2, 3, 4, 5, 6, 7, 8, 9, 10). When you arrive at the top of the mountain, allow yourselves a few moments to focus on your breath and slowly, when you are ready, open your eyes.

Conclude with one minute of contemplative silence.

Air ~ East ~ Spring ~ Truth

INVOKING THE ELEMENT AIR

"There arises a spirituality in which the human city is human not simply by the fact that it is made up of persons and institutions; plants, the water, the pure air, the animals, and healthy conditions of natural life are also about to be brought together in harmony." (Boff 1993:107)

(This meditation is best done outside; choose a place where you can stand for five minutes and do the invocation. If doing this in a group, listen to the directions from the Leader.)

Begin with three minutes of contemplative silence followed by Acknowledgment of Country.

Leader: Face the direction of the East where the sun gives light and raise your arms to welcome the sun wherever she is in the sky.

Close your eyes and feel the ground beneath your feet. Raise your hands again and this time take a deep breath in; hold and then let the breath all the way out.

Sway your arms across your body from side to side all the while looking up at the sky. Keep breathing and keep your eyes open.

Say in your mind "I invoke air… air I am… I breathe in air and I breathe out air."

Take your right hand and tap firmly all the way down your left side.

Take your left hand and tap firmly all the way down your right side.

Say in your mind: "Air I am… I breathe in air and I breathe out air."

Turn to the left and raise your hands to greet the day.

Turn to your right and raise your hands to invoke the gift of air.

Turn behind you and raise your hands and be grateful for air.

Turn to the front and bow your head and breathe in and out the fresh air.

Leader: Repeat after me in your mind:

Creating, Energising Great Spirit present in all that is

I breathe in and out waking up to all that is

My heart and imagination alert and present

I breathe in and out waking up to all that is. Amen.

Conclude with one minute of contemplative silence.

Air ~ East ~ Spring ~ Truth

CLIMATE EMERGENCY

"We're reaching a fork in the road; two paths are diverging on planet Earth, and the one we choose will make all the difference for the life of the planet. Shall we continue our medieval religious practices in a medieval paradigm and mechanistic culture and undergo extinction? Or shall we wake up to this dynamic, evolutionary universe and the rise of consciousness toward an integral wholeness?" (Ilia Delio 2013:4)

Watch Greta Thunberg on https://youtu.be/RjsLm5PCdVQ to warm up to this ritual.

Begin with three minutes of contemplative silence followed by Acknowledgment of Country.

"I have the power, presence and possibility to make a difference." (Whispered mantra)

Reflect: "Right now we are facing a man-made disaster of global scale. Our greatest threat in thousands of years is climate change. If we don't take action, the collapse of our civilizations and the extinction of much of the natural world is on the horizon." David Attenborough BBC News 3/12/18

Climate Emergency Pledge

I pledge to read ten minutes every day, if I haven't already done so, about what climate scientists are saying about climate emergency.

I pledge to read *Laudato Si'* Chapter One "What is happening to our Common Home?"

I pledge to google what groups in my local area are working to combat climate emergency.

One minute of contemplative silence.

Pray Psalm 148 (adapted)

> Praise, all you shining stars!
>
> Praise, waters, sea creatures and all deeps!
>
> Praise, fire and hail, snow and mist, and stormy winds!
>
> Praise, mountains, and all hills, fruit trees and cedars!
>
> Praise, animals and livestock, creeping things and flying birds!

All in the earth community are threatened by this climate emergency.

If you have the time: this longer YouTube by Greta Thunberg is worth reflecting on - https://youtu.be/EAmmUIEsN9A

Conclude with one minute of contemplative silence.

Air ~ East ~ Spring ~ Truth

PEACE

"Grace… opens up the mystery within which we live, and move and have our being. From within that spacious, grace filled landscape, we embrace God's gracious embodiment in the midst of creation." (Diarmuid O'Murchu 2017:40)

Begin with three minutes of contemplative silence followed by Acknowledgment of Country.

Watch this YouTube **Deep Peace** by Sarah Thomsen to warm up to this ritual: https://youtu.be/kb-FAOe396U

Sit in a quiet place outside where you will not be disturbed. This meditation offers you a brief space to be still with fresh air, breeze and light surrounding you. Take some deep breaths and open yourself to the mystery of all that is within you and outside of you.

Breathing in and breathing out, calm your mind and let go of any thoughts that hinder you from being present to this moment. If thoughts arise, allow them to pass through and let them go.

Breathe in the peacefulness of this moment… breathe out any tension.

Breathe in the peace of the trees that surround you… breathe out any worries.

Breathe in the peace of earth under your feet… breathe out anxiety.

Breathe in the peace of this moment; this is a new moment… breathe out unwanted thoughts.

Breathe in peace, deep peace and relax… breathe out any tension.

Breathe peace into all your loved ones.

Breathe peace into your dreams now and into the future.

Breathe peace into yourself, deep peace, and breathe out fear.

Breathe peace into all four corners of earth: north, south, west and east.

Filled with a peaceful stance and grateful for the gift of grace and peace I pray:

> Every day of this my life;
> Faithful Presence lies within!
> In the morning light – my heart
> Now pounds gratefully in tune;
> Peace flows gently through me now
> In the morning light – my heart
> Now pounds gratefully in tune;
> Peace flows gently through me now. Amen.

Conclude with one minute of contemplative silence.

Air ~ East ~ Spring ~ Truth

A MEDITATION ON AIR

"Just as the sun illuminates the air and shines through it, but keeps its source for itself, so You pour all pleasure and every delight into every one of your creatures – and into me – and yet You keep the root of pleasure and guard delight's essence in Yourself so that I might seek You as the ever-giving source of what gives true pleasure and lasting delight."
(Sweeney and Burrows 2017:127)

Begin with three minutes of contemplative silence followed by Acknowledgment of Country. If possible, sit outside where you can feel the breeze and fresh air. Sit for a few moments in silence and close your eyes; become aware of your breathing and draw in a number of deep breaths. You may like to use the Sufi Air Breath which is to breathe through your mouth and out through your mouth.

As you remain relaxed and aware, breathing naturally and rhythmically, read one at a time a quotation on air written by David Suzuki. (Used with permission)

> Air is our element,
>
> We live inside the atmosphere,
>
> The envelope of mixed gases that forms the outer layer of the planet,
>
> We are more than just air breathers;
>
> We are creatures made for and by the substance we need every minute of our lives.
>
> And just as air has shaped and sustained living beings, so living beings created and still sustain the air.
>
> Air is a physical substance;
>
> It embraces us so intimately that it is hard to say where we leave off and air begins.
>
> Into the centre of our being, deep into the moist,
>
> Delicate membranous labyrinth within our chests, and putting it to use.
>
> Invisible and indivisible, air is a place without borders or owners,
>
> Shared by all life on Earth.

Each one of us, past, present and future, needs air every minute of every day we live,
Every breath is a sacrament, an essential ritual. As we imbibe this sacred element, we are physically linked to all of our present biological relatives. (David Suzuki)
Conclude with a minute of contemplative silence and five Sufi Air Breaths.

Air ~ East ~ Spring ~ Truth

EXTINCTION OF SPECIES: A SORROWFUL MOMENT IN TIME

"The publication in Paris of the Global Assessment Report on 6th May, 2019, confirmed that we are now living in the sixth largest extinction in 3.8 billion years of Earth's history. The 1,800-page study shows that we and future generation of species are seriously at risk, unless firm action is taken to reverse this trend. The last time such a major extinction of life happened on Earth was 65 million years ago when an asteroid crashed into the Yucatan area of Mexico. The explosion caused such global destruction that more than half the species on earth became extinct." (Sean McDonagh, in *The Universe,* 2019)

Begin with three minutes of contemplative silence followed by Acknowledgment of Country.
Song: *Om Shanti Om (Peace)* Deva Premal Mantras for Precarious Times. Streaming on Apple Music and Spotify.
After listening to the mantra for four minutes, sit in silence and bring to mind the import of the Global Assessment Report on the risk of extinction of over a million species.
Read these words out aloud to yourself:
"The report states that the human footprint on our planet is so large now that it is not allowing enough space for other species to exist or flourish. The authors believe that one million species are at risk of extinction in the next two to three decades. Consequently, the annihilation of wildlife by human activity is eroding the very foundations of human civilization. The abundance of native species in most major land habitats has fallen by a fifth since 1990. For example, frogs and amphibians have suffered a horrendous 40 per cent decline. The biomass of wild animals has fallen by a staggering 82 percent." (Sean McDonagh)
Song: Play again *Om Shanti Om (Peace)* Deva Premal.

Litany of Lament
Frogs and amphibians we remember and we are listening. We lament.
Natural Eco-Systems and Rainforests we remember and we are listening. We lament.
Cavendish Bananas we remember and we are listening. We lament.
Coral Reefs and marine mammals we remember and we are listening. We lament.
Destruction of biodiversity we remember and we are listening. We lament.
Song: Play again *Om Shanti Om (Peace)* Deva Premal.

Prayer for all Species: Loving kindness in me wells up in empathy for this devastating sadness and I commit to create a daily practice to remember, listen and act for all species.

Conclude with a minute of contemplative silence.

Air ~ East ~ Spring ~ Truth

BREATHE LOVE

"The ecological crises of water, heat, loss of species, degradation of Earth, etc. are evidence that our communal sense of place is awry… each of us can have a role as teachers, grandparents, artists and poets, healers and professionals etc. to bring about reconciliation between ourselves and the planetary system we call home." (Trevor Parton: 2019)

Song: *Breathe Love* Susan Lincoln & Craig Toungate, available on Apple Music and Spotify.
Sit outside in a quiet place where you will not be interrupted for ten minutes.
Listen to the song and take three minutes of contemplative silence.
Place your left hand on your heart and your right hand on top of your left hand.
Attune to the sounds around you; the air; the light; the atmosphere and feel your heart awakening to your surrounds.

Breathe in Loving Kindness Breathe out Loving Kindness to all in your street.

Breathe in Loving Kindness Breathe out Loving kindness to all in your town and city.

Breathe in Loving Kindness Breathe out Loving Kindness to all in your State.

Breathe in Loving Kindness Breathe out Loving Kindness to all in your Country.

Breathe in Loving Kindness Breathe out Loving Kindness to all beings and all species.

Breathe in Loving Kindness Breathe out Loving Kindness to earth, air, fire and water.

Breathe in Loving Kindness Breathe out Loving Kindness to every living heart in the world.

Attune to the sounds around you; the air; the light; the atmosphere and feel your heart awakened and radiant with vibrant presence to all that is.

A Blessing for Mother Earth (used with permission Trevor Parton)
Finally humanity is beginning to perceive that our planet is a living being which has been infinitely patient with the abuse we have wrought upon it.
We bless Mother Earth in its infinite abundance and stunning beauty, the wealth of the fauna and flora, the infinite subtlety of its growth and survival mechanisms and its mission of supporting the human race. We bless Mother Earth in its soils everywhere and their ability to recover their original integrity. We bless the numerous animal and plant species and their ability to resist all attacks on their habitat, be it through overgrazing, overfishing, deforestation or some other form of abuse. Amen,

Conclude with one minute of contemplative silence.

ELEMENT: WATER

DIRECTION: NORTH

SEASON: SUMMER

GIFT: LOVE

Water ~ North ~ Summer ~ Love

WALKING MEDITATION FOR RECONCILIATION

"Every aspect of the human, including the human mind, is as much Earth as the mountains, rivers, animals, birds and other wonders of the Earth Community" (Sean McDonagh 1986:80)

Song: *Aboriginal Earth Chants: Uluru – Monument to Time (Apple Music)*

Begin with three minutes of contemplative silence and Acknowledgment of Country.

Take several deep breaths.

If you are praying this ritual alone, walk mindfully whilst listening to the music for eight minutes.

If you are with others, gather in a circle and listen together to *Uluru – Monument to Time*
And then gradually walk as the music plays for eight minutes, noticing all the elements around you especially sounds and species that fly and sing.
Gather afterwards in a circle on the ground or in chairs.

Leader: We are gathering to remember the First Peoples who have shown people how to love land and care for it. We acknowledge them today and pay respects to elders living, those who have died and those who are to come.

Leader: "There can be no reconciliation without justice."

All: We take responsibility to create justice.

Leader: "There can be no justice without understanding."

All: We take responsibility to deepen our understanding.

Leader: "There can be no understanding without standing in the shoes of another."

All: We are choosing to learn how to stand in the shoes of another and role reverse.

Leader: "There can be no understanding without being still."

All: We are creating time for stillness.

Sharing: After silence, the group is invited one by one to share what is emerging. What is arising now? There is a pause after each one before the next person speaks.

Conclude with one minute of contemplative silence.

Water ~ North ~ Summer ~ Love

A MEDITATION ON PRESENCE

"The Earth of humankind contains all moisture, all verdancy, and all germinating power. It is in so many ways Fruitful. All creation comes from it." **(Gabriele Uhlein, 1982:58)**

Song: "*The Presence You Are*" Streaming on Apple Music or Spotify.

Begin with three minutes of contemplative silence and Acknowledgment of Country.

If at all possible, this ritual is celebrated in darkness with the sound of running water in the background. You will also need a votive candle for each person. These can be lit beforehand.

Gather in a circle with the votive candles burning.

Listen to the Song: *The Presence You Are.*
It's not what you do, but how you do it.
It's not what you see, but how you see.
It's not what you say, what you know or achieve,
but it's the Presence, the Presence you are.
  © 2006 by Jan Novotka's Music, LLC (ASCAP). All rights reserved.

Sit in contemplative silence for five minutes and let the song words drop into a place within you where you feel most still and quiet. As you breathe in and out, allow the words of the song to play over in your mind. "The Presence You Are."

Leader: As you take a few deep breaths, open your eyes and focus on the candles. Gradually, take your awareness to the candle closest to you and allow the flickering flame at the centre of the wick to invite you into a reflection on yourself as a sacred tabernacle, holding Presence. Great Spirit dwells within you; flows through you; leads and guides you.

Leader: It's not what you do;

All: It's how we do it.

Leader: It's not what you see;

All: It's how we see.

Leader: It's not what you say;

All: It's the Presence we are.

Conclude with one minute of contemplative silence.

Water ~ North ~ Summer ~ Love

COSMIC WALK

"This story has the power to awaken us more deeply to who we are. For just as the Milky Way is the universe in the form of a galaxy, and an orchid is the universe in the form of a flower, we are the universe in the form of a human. And every time we are drawn to look up into the night sky and reflect on the awesome beauty of the universe, we are actually the universe reflecting on itself. And this changes everything." (Brian Swimme, Mary Evelyn Tucker 2011:2)

(There are many versions of the *Cosmic Walk* first written by Miriam McGillis OP. A Google search will bring up many for you to choose from.) The *Cosmic Walk* is a powerful ritual that tells the Great Story of our shared existence. It invokes a sense of sacredness of Earth in our 13.8 billion year history.

Best celebrated outside and with a large spiral rope depicting the unfolding of the Universe Story, and battery operated candles may be placed as the narrator tells the story.

I suggest that you print off this version http://www.thegreatstory.org/CosmicWalk.pdf

If you are choosing a night cosmic walk using darkness and only candlelight, it is best celebrated inside.

If you choose to enact the ritual outside and then return to the main room where you are meeting.

Begin with three minutes of contemplative silence and Acknowledgment of Country.

Watch the suggested YouTube.https://youtu.be/wauTegRZ6KE *A Child of The Universe* sung by John Seed at Moon Court 2012

The song was written by Theo Simons https://en.wikipedia.org/wiki/Seize_the_Day_(band)

The lyrics may be found https://lyricstranslate.com/en/rainbow-songs-child-universe-lyrics.html

Seated in a circle a time of contemplative silence allows for the incredible gift of the evolving unfolding of the universe. A candle is passed around the circle and as each person holds the candle they give thanks for a part of the Cosmic Walk.

All: Psalm 148 (adapted)

Praise be Divine Presence, in the heights, in the sun and moon.

In the waters, in all sea creatures, fire and hail, snow and mist, in mountains and hills fruit trees and all cedars, beasts and all livestock, creeping things and flying birds, in the stars and galaxies, breath of our breath and the very heart of our heart. Praise!

Conclude with one minute of contemplative silence.

Water ~ North ~ Summer ~ Love

COMMUNITY EARTH RITUAL: SUMMER SOLSTICE

"Summer Solstice is a good time to contemplate how the Sun is in all we are and do, all that we eat and drink – that it is the sun in us, that has ripened, that is in our every thought and action. We are the Sun, coming to Fullness in its creative engagement with Earth." (Glenys Livingstone 2008:296)

This is a link to Glenys Livingstone's website and there you can purchase the summer meditation https://pagaian.org/pagaian-prayers-invoking-her/ A google search for summer solstice resources such as YouTubes and music and dance will provide a good background for the ritual.

A Possible Process for Creating a Ritual – Remote Preparation
For several years, a community group has been meeting to welcome summer and create a ritual together.
Two weeks before the scheduled ritual, an email is sent to the group to remind them to reflect on summer and allow their contemplative stance to flow freely.
"For those of you who are coming for the first time we have been working with the idea of a 'contemplative stance' – allowing anything that emerges in us as summer nears - thought; idea; action; musing; daydreaming; synchronicity, etc. to make a note and bring something to celebrate this at the summer solstice ritual. We will celebrate with whatever you bring to contribute to the ritual – out of your reflections since the last ritual – poetry; music; sacred space décor; symbols; readings; movement; drama, dance; and art works."

Suggested Process for Creating a Ritual on the Day
Gather in a circle and acknowledge the land and original ancestors.
Begin with three minutes of contemplative silence.
The leader invites each person one by one to share what they have brought to the ritual.
The listening process is discerning and appreciative.
Using contemplative listening (one person speaks at a time and whatever is suggested is accepted without interruption or disagreement), the group then suggests possible placing of the texts, décor, music, dance, etc. This usually works out smoothly and with great respect for the gifts shared among the group.
The ritual is enacted.
Conclude with one minute of contemplative silence.

Water ~ North ~ Summer ~ Love

THE CLOUDS

"**Where are the places you hold most sacred? Is there a special place you once visited on a journey, maybe where you fell in love for the first time? Perhaps your home is sacred to you – quiet moments spent by the fire, or the liveliness of family and friends. Is it the ocean? A forest? A monastery? Our sacred places give us refuge and we know them intimately. To see a place we love desecrated or irrevocably changed can be heartbreaking. Often, we will do anything we can to protect and take care of a place sacred to us.**"
(*Kosmos* Journal: 2018)
(A bowl of water is placed in the centre of the circle and a towel, Prepare a copy of the poem for everyone.)

Begin with three minutes of contemplative silence and Acknowledgment of Country.

Leader: Today we will adapt *Lectio Divina* to reflect on this poem by Trevor Parton (used with permission) and as we gather in this circle let us listen to a reading of the poem.
"*Lectio Divina*… is an ancient practice and can include any sacred text – a passage that moves you, a poem you love, or an image that is calling for your attention." (Christine Valters Paintner 2011:18)

> I am bacteria that lives
> In the leaves of rainforest trees.
> I float in water vapour
> That the leaves transpire daily.
> I rise in the sky above,
> Where I meet clouds,
> And increase their fluffy masses.
> Eventually I gather around me
> Lots of condensing water,
> And I return to the forest as rain –
> My job done.
> This is my exciting life,
> And I've been doing this for millions of years.
> Please don't chop down my life.

Leader: Let us listen to the poem being read again and this time you will be invited to share one word that stays with you.

Circle sharing with pauses to allow slowing down, becoming fully present, and maintaining a sense of awe and wonder as each one speaks.

Leader: Let us listen to the poem for a third time and you are asked to listen for an invitation that stays with you.

Circle sharing with pauses to allow slowing down, becoming fully present, and maintaining a sense of awe and wonder as each one speaks.

Group Sharing: In groups of three, share favourite images and metaphors from this poem and what you are being invited to allow to emerge in your own life.

Leader: This bowl of water is precious and links us to our origins. Our bodies are largely made up of water. We cannot live without water. Water is sacramental and sustains and nourishes as well as cleanses. Today we will honour this bowl of water and in the words of the poem remember that "*This is my exciting life, and I've been doing this for millions of years.*"

Awake to our senses of appreciation, we acknowledge "As air is sacred gas, so is water a sacred liquid that links us to all the oceans of the world and ties us back in time to the very birthplace of all life." (David Suzuki 1997: 75)

As the bowl of water is brought around the circle, the person next to you has his/her hands washed and dried before moving onto the next person. After the hands are washed and dried, the person prays aloud gratitude for the gift of water and in particular… When all have had their hands washed and dried and prayers of gratitude have been prayed, the gathered group recites slowly the poem.

> I am bacteria that lives
> In the leaves of rainforest trees.
> I float in water vapour
> That the leaves transpire daily.
> I rise in the sky above,
> Where I meet clouds,
> And increase their fluffy masses.
> Eventually I gather around me
> Lots of condensing water,
> And I return to the forest as rain –
> My job done.
> This is my exciting life,
> And I've been doing this for millions of years.
> Please don't chop down my life.

Conclude with one minute of contemplative silence.

Water ~ North ~ Summer ~ Love

OCEAN SUNDAY

"Like a saturated sponge, creation is dripping wet with divine presence, so to speak. Like a soaking ocean, a flowing fountain, an inexhaustible wellspring of sweet water, the life of the Spirit pervades the world." (Elizabeth Johnson 2014:137)

Song: Chants: Ritual Music – *The Beginning of the Earth* Streamed on Apple Music and Spotify.

(Adapted with permission www.normanhabel.com/)

A collection of shells and sea water together with images of the ocean could be used in this ritual. Each person chooses one as they take their seat in the circle prepared.

Begin with three minutes of contemplative silence and Acknowledgment of Country.

Welcome!

We share our ritual with the oceans of Earth, created by the Wisdom of God. We join the Psalmists and call the sea to roar with songs of praise. We sing with the seven seas and celebrate the wondrous creatures of the watery deep. With our Creator, we rejoice with whales, dolphins and other 'sea creatures'. With the Spirit, we groan with animal species and humans that are suffering from our human acts of pollution.

Background

"Ocean refers to the masses of waters that cover two thirds of Earth's surface, along with the seven seas and the watery deeps where a myriad of species live, many of which are still undiscovered. The ocean is a world of mystery and beauty, of fascinating depths and spectacular life forms. The ocean is that vast domain many of our ancestors crossed to reach all parts of planet Earth. The waters of the oceans are the waters of life for the entire planet."

Leader: In the name of the Spirit of God
who hovered over the primal waters.
In the name of the Word of God
who parted the waters for Earth to appear.
In the name of the Wisdom of God,
who filled the deep with amazing design! Amen.

All: **Holy! Holy! Holy!**
The oceans are filled with God's presence.

Leader: Take the symbol you received at the door, hold it in your hand and share with the person next to you a special memory of times at the seashore or on the water that stirred your spirit or sense of wonder.

All: Thank you, Great Spirit, for the oceans,
living waters that are part of our life on Earth.

Water ~ North ~ Summer ~ Love

Lament

Leader: We have become alienated from Earth
and viewed this planet as disposable,
a source of endless resources,
and no consideration of those who are to come.

Leader: We are sorry.
We have polluted Earth's waters with toxins;
We have killed millions of species in the ocean.
We have turned our greed into global warming.
We have helped cause arctic regions to melt.
We have devalued human life.
We have loved progress more than the planet.
We are sorry. We are sorry.

Psalm: Psalm 104:24-26 'A World Created by Wisdom'

The whole world is formed by the Wisdom of God, thereby giving it all its integral parts, laws, design, and purpose. That world even includes domains where God 'plays' with wild creatures in the ocean.

Leader: "Earth is full of your creatures; yonder is the sea, great and wide, creeping things innumerable are there; living things both small and great." Psalm 104:24-26

Leader: Take three minutes of silence, pondering on all the sea creatures that you know of or have seen.

Creed: We believe Earth is a sanctuary,
a sacred planet filled with God's presence,
a home for us to share with our kin.
We believe that God became flesh and blood,
became a part of Earth,
a human being called Jesus Christ,
who lived and breathed and spoke among us.
We believe that the risen Jesus
is the Christ at the core of creation
reconciling all things to God,
renewing all creation and filling the universe.
We believe the Spirit renews life in creation
groans in empathy with a suffering creation,
and waits with us for the rebirth of creation.
We believe that with Christ we will rise
and with Christ we will celebrate a new creation.

Conclude with one minute of contemplative silence.

Water ~ North ~ Summer ~ Love

I AM A SPRING

"The history of our friendship with God is always linked to particular places which take on an intensely personal meaning; we remember places, and revisiting those memories, does us much good." (LS 84)

YouTube Link: A Grateful Day https://youtu.be/zSt7k_q_qRU David Steindal-Rast

Poem: *Spiral Flows – Spring* used with permission Neil Davidson.

This ritual is best done outside where, with a device, you can watch the five minute YouTube on gratitude.

Begin with three minutes of contemplative silence and Acknowledgment of Country.

Meditation: Take several deep breaths and focus on the area outside where you are sitting. Watch for any signs of life.

Each time you focus on a creature or a plant or shrub, bow to each one separately and say in your mind's eye "For you I am grateful".

You may like to go one step further and bow profoundly and with your hands joined say in your mind's eye "Namaste" – "I bow to the divinity in you and when you are in that place and I am in that place we are one"

To conclude this meditation you may like to slowly ponder on the poem.

"Earth Speaks to *me* through others and *through* me to others
Others see Earth speak through me I am a pure irresistible force of life-giving energy
I am a pure source from deep within Earth herself
Deep reserves of potential finding beautiful ways to surface
I join drops into pools and then into flows
Spiral flows to heal and renew
While needed I will flow
I am a spring."

    Neil Davidson June 2017

Prayer of Gratitude: I give thanks for Earth for pools; for springs; for fresh cold water, for oceans, rivers, and lakes. I give thanks for those I know and for those I am yet to get to know. Amen.

Conclude with one minute of contemplative silence.

Water ~ North ~ Summer ~ Love

A LITANY FOR BIRDS

"The Canadian bishops rightly pointed out that no creature is excluded from this manifestation of God: From panoramic vistas to the tiniest living form, nature is a constant source of wonder and awe." (LS: 85)

Song: Melissa Philippe, *You Are Not Alone* – streaming on Apple Music and Spotify

Begin with three minutes of contemplative silence followed by Acknowledgment of Country.

This is a walking meditation and can be prayed anywhere outdoors.

You will need this book and a device to play the music.

Say aloud each *blessed* and echo the *blessed* as you walk.

> Blessed be birds evolved 54 million years ago – echo
> Blessed be birdsong – echo
> Blessed be small birds and large birds – echo
> Blessed be nesting birds – echo
> Blessed be magpies – echo
> Blessed be all endangered birds – echo
> Blessed be all birds choosing to travel long distances –echo
> Blessed be cockatoos – echo
> Blessed be plovers – echo
> Blessed be brolgas –echo
> Blessed be kookaburras – echo

Listen to the song as you walk and be aware of your gratitude for the trees that are home to the birds, as well as the seeds that feed them.

Prayer: Praise Be! Consciousness and awareness grow in me so that I respect and value all species, especially birds that are critical for ecological balance. Praise Be! Great Spirit coursing through all that is, I vow to become more aware and more loving toward all species. Praise Be!

Conclude with one minute of contemplative silence.

Water ~ North ~ Summer ~ Love

WE GIVE THANKS

"The skies that enchant us, the lands that embrace us, have memorised the chapters of Earth time. These chapters are written into mountains, valleys, forests, bush land, deserts, rivers, flood plains and lapping seas. The genes in our bodies record the memory of the evolutionary story of life, and through the food we eat we enter into the mystery of a communion that holds the origin of all life." (*Earthsong* Journal Anne Boyd 2009:1)

Song: Betsy Rose – Sacred Ground *Mother Earth* Streaming Apple Music and Spotify

Gratitude Prayer of Thanks: *In this food we fully realise the presence of the entire universe supporting our existence.* (Used with permission, Jim Casey.)

Pat Long writes about **Eating Mindfully: Embracing the hunger of the universe.** In this ritual, you are invited to reflect meditatively on the daily gifts of food and how Earth sustains us.

For this ritual you will need a piece of fruit cut up and ready for eating.

Begin with three minutes of contemplative silence followed by Acknowledgment of Country.

Sit outside in a garden, orchard or edible forest and contemplate the lifecycle of a seed.

Eat a piece of the fruit and, as you do, say these words *In this food we fully realise the presence of the entire universe supporting our existence* and give thanks for the deliciousness of the fruit. The taste, such a gift is taste.

Read slowly "The act of eating brings me into direct contact with this unbroken chain of transformations from the beginning of space and time. The iron in my blood, the calcium in my bones, the oxygen in my brain, is the same iron and calcium and oxygen formed in the supernova explosions. The light energy captured in the vegetables I eat is a transformation of the original light." Pat Long: 2009

Listen to the song *Mother Earth*.

Eat another piece of fruit and, as you do, say these words *In this food we fully realise the presence of the entire universe supporting our existence.*

Read Slowly "How much of my food can be locally sourced and grown organically? In addition to my own backyard, what opportunities are there for growing food in the neighbourhood? Where are the local permaculture designed farms and gardens? What can I learn from then and how might I become involved in this system?" Pat Long: 2009

Eat your final piece of fruit and, as you do, say these words *In this food we fully realise the presence of the entire universe supporting our existence.*

Conclude with one minute of contemplative silence.

Water ~ North ~ Summer ~ Love

JESUS BY THE LAKE

"Without minimizing the social and political aspects of the kingdom of God, it is very important to see that the *reign of God is the presence of God within us…*In a profound sense *the reign of God unfolds as the holy web that binds us all to each other and to all of creation.*" **(Cletus Wessels 2000:152)**

Begin with three minutes of contemplative silence and Acknowledgment of Country.

Song: *Early Morning Songbirds in* Journey to Australia Vol 2 streaming on apple Music and Spotify.

Listen to this song as you read the phrases below.

Meditation: Human like Us. (This response by Michael Morwood is used with permission.)

(Sit in a solitary place outside and reflect on these words, praying them slowly and mindfully.)

Jesus, human like us you enjoyed walking by the Lake.

Jesus, human like us you enjoyed.

Jesus, human like us you went out on the boat and fished.

Jesus, human like us you enjoyed.

Jesus, you took time to go to the lake by yourself and meditate.

Jesus, human like us you took time out.

Jesus, you ate with friends and strangers alike.

Jesus, you called for change and transformation of unjust structures.

Jesus, you are way, truth and life.

Jesus, you revealed the Spirit of Life.

Jesus, you opened hearts and minds up to prophetic justice.

You brought light, love and justice.

To conclude this reflection: A journal idea: Which of the statements touches your own experience most deeply? Which of them felt as if it were calling you home?

Conclude with one minute of contemplative silence.

Water ~ North ~ Summer ~ Love

STONE FLOWS TO WATER

"One thing that we can do is connect deeply with the story of our living Earth on a daily basis. This alone helps to elevate our consciousness, right? The more we can work on behalf of Life where we live, the more we build community, the more we build a practice of global citizenship…*practices* that bring us closer each day to the reality of our Interbeing." (Rhonda Fabian: 2018 https://www.kosmosjournal.org/kj_article/on-elevating-the-narrative/)

Song: *Stone Flows to Water* Murray Kyle https://murraykyle.bandcamp.com/track/stone-flows-to-water used with permission.

In the setting, there is a bowl of stones in water.

Begin with three minutes of contemplative silence and Acknowledgment of Country.

Gather in a circle and listen to *Stone Flows to Water* as one person walks into the centre of the circle, and picks up the bowl of stones which are in water, inviting each person to choose a stone.

Leader: The stone you are holding has a history and it has been said that even the smallest stone in a riverbed has the entire history of the universe inscribed upon it. (Okuizumi 2000:1)

Pause for reflection.

Leader: Close your eyes and take a few deep breaths; and then open your eyes and gaze at the stone. "34 million years ago, complete separation between Antarctica and Australia had occurred in the Southern Ocean." (Philomena Manifold 2017:14) The history of this little stone carries the memory of that time. Allow the water on the stone to cool you.

Close your eyes again and imagine the shape and colour of the stone.

With your eyes closed, prepare now for a guided meditation on the season of summer, remaining aware of the stone in your hand.

Summer is a time of sunshine and fruiting – a time for us, in Australia, for so many fruits. Stone fruits – peaches, plums, nectarines, cherries and berries of many kinds; in more tropical climes, there are especially watermelons, pawpaws, mangoes, pineapples and bananas. We are truly blessed with the fruits of summer.

Summer, especially in a dry land like Australia, is a time which highlights the significance of water for life. We welcome rain in time of drought and dread of bushfires. We welcome the coolness of the surf in the sea or a swim in the pool. We relish the cleanliness of a shower, the cool drink of water on a hot day. We do not take water for granted – it is gift.

Water ~ North ~ Summer ~ Love

In every part of the world, certain springs or rivers or lakes or other sources of water were – or are – regarded as sacred places. People came – or come – to these places on pilgrimage, and for healing.

Let us pause for some quiet reflective time, keeping our eyes closed. Holding the small stone, become aware of the summer images – what fruits of your artistic imagination have come to fruit this year? What things have prevented their full ripening? What may be blemishes on their skin or within their flesh? Even at the core? What fruits would you like to have seen blossom and ripen on the tree of your year's life, but found that they did not? Perhaps after this meditation, you may like to journal your response to these questions.

In your imagination now, place your prayers and wishes for your life into the stone that you are holding. May this stone be a reminder to you of your creativity and your capacity for expressing your artistic imagination? *Pause.*

In your own time, open your eyes and gaze at the stone, acknowledging that this stone carries ancient history.

Leader: We will now make a circle of stones as I read the following:

"One thing that we can do is connect deeply with the story of our living Earth on a daily basis. This alone helps to elevate our consciousness, right? The more we can work on behalf of Life where we live, the more we build community, the more we build a practice of global citizenship… *practices* that bring us closer each day to the reality of our Interbeing." (Rhonda Fabian: 2018 https://www.kosmosjournal.org/kj_article/on-elevating-the-narrative/)

When the circle of stones is complete, there will be time for contemplative listening.

Each person makes a response to the question "What fruits can I bring to practising community-building and assisting others to become aware of the interconnectedness of all that is?"

After each person speaks, there will be a pause before the next person speaks. There is no discussion or interaction – simply deep listening.

After the contemplative listening is completed, the stones are picked up and silently returned to the bowl of water.

Conclude with one minute of contemplative silence.

Water ~ North ~ Summer ~ Love

PROTECTING THE WATER BODIES OF THE WORLD

"The first voice in Laudato Si' comes from the Ecumenical Patriarch Bartholomew, who since his election as patriarch in 1991, has constantly focused on protecting God's creation, especially the water bodies of the world." (Sean McDonagh 2017:11)

This ritual will work well by the ocean which in most parts of the world is being severely polluted by plastic and other unwanted debris. People are asked to bring buckets and gloves to clean up the rubbish that is being left by the waterways. Tibetan bells will also be useful. Begin with three minutes of contemplative silence and Acknowledgment of Country.

Reader:
We all depend on the oceans, the planet's last great wilderness, for our very existence. They feed billions of people, regulate the weather, and control natural and atmospheric systems.
Most of the world's existing basic forms of life first appeared in the seas some 550 million years ago, and even now many new species probably live undiscovered in the ocean depths. In some ways, life is even more diverse at sea than on land.
Dr Thilo Bode is International Executive Director of Greenpeace.

> **Chime bar** or Centering Prayer App with bell tones and timer.

Reader: Seas of Change

THE ECUMENICAL THRONE OF ORTHODOXY, as preserver and herald of the ancient Patristic tradition and of the rich liturgical experience of the Christian Church, witnesses with great sorrow the exhaustion of our planet's biologically rich marine resources: the over exploitation of the world's fisheries and the by-catch of threatened marine species; pollution and eutrophication of coastal waters that are choking the seas; the destruction of coastal habitats, accounting for the loss of productive ecosystems; the invasion of exotic species upsetting the delicate balance of the oceanic web of life; and the change of the global climate that has already been implicated in algae blooms and coral reef destruction. Nowadays the oceans of the world are a sea of tears.

At the Phanar, March 21, 1998
Your fervent supplicant before God Creator of all, the Ecumenical Patriarch
BARTHOLOMEW OF CONSTANTINOPLE

> **Chime bar** or Centering Prayer App with bell tones and timer.

For the next fifteen minutes each person takes their bucket and gloves to collect pollution on the sands and in the dunes.

> **Chime bar** or Centering Prayer App with bell tones and timer.

Conclude with one minute of contemplative silence whilst looking out to sea.

Water ~ North ~ Summer ~ Love

SUMMER MANDALA

"Let the sacred period of late summer teach us the virtues of contentment and at-homeness with its multi-coloured riches. Let it teach us to take stock of what we have given and received, to know that these are enough. May it open us to delight in the abundance of life." **(Diann L. Neu 2002:106)**

Begin with three minutes of contemplative silence followed by Acknowledgment of Country.

Watch this YouTube as a warm-up to creating your summer mandala.

https://youtu.be/cMNwYBUbXF4 This *Song of Community* by Carolyn McDade is sung by an 11 year old.

Place a circular plate or tray in front of you and slowly, in concentric circles, add leaves; shells; flowers; petals; small pebbles; and fresh herbs.

Follow with three minutes of contemplative silence.

Mandala Reflection

Relax into your breath now; giving time for peace and quiet.

Ponder on your plate or tray; giving time for peace and quiet.

Reflection Reading: "… nothing in our genes was present a year ago. The tissue in our stomach renews itself weekly, the skin is shed monthly, and the liver regenerated every six weeks. Every moment, a portion of the body's trillions of atoms is dissipating to the world outside, and ninety-eight percent of them are replaced annually. Each time we breathe, we take in a quadrillion atoms breathed by the rest of humanity within the last two weeks, and more than a million atoms breathed personally sometime by each person on earth." David S. Toolan SJ (2001: 188)

Every fourth breath that you take along with every person on the planet is dependent on the Amazon forest. Every third breath you take along with every person on the planet is dependent on the Oceans.

Give thanks for this miracle and then proceed to do the Sufi Water Breath several times.

Inhale through the nose and exhale through the mouth.

At every third breath, give thanks for the Oceans.

Count every fourth breath and give thanks for the Amazon forest.

When you come to the end of the breaths take one more look of appreciation at your summer mandala and before returning the mandala to earth.

Conclude with one minute of contemplative silence.

Water ~ North ~ Summer ~ Love

CARING FOR OUR COMMON HOME

"Entering authentically and critically into what is happening to our common home and humbly acknowledging our human implication in today's ecological crisis can only be possible by consciously entering our heart space, by coming home in a primal sense. In the sanctity of our deepest selves we are nudged to be awake and attentive to our intrinsic wholesomeness and to the beauty and complexity of life as it unfolds." (Nellie McLaughlin 2015: 19)

Begin with three minutes of contemplative silence and Acknowledgment of Country.

This ritual is offered as a group ritual. Gather outside around a bird bath; large bowl of water; or a pond. You will also need a copy of this book.

Leader: We are gathered on sacred ground, where we are sitting is sacred, this is sacred ground and we are sacred. This water we are gathered around is sacred. We remember and call to mind the wonderful story of long ago, when Great Spirit hovered on the waters and gave meaning to the chaos, and life to all creatures of earth. Let us now enter into silence.

All: We enter knowingly and willingly into silence around this sacred water.

After three minutes of contemplative silence the following phrases are read out. They are by David Suzuki (*The Sacred Balance*, used with permission) A member of the group reads the phrases.

Water is the raw material of creation, the source of life…

When the waters break, the child is born from them…

Water is at the heart of human ritual…

Baptism often welcomes the child into the human family…

The powerful symbolism of water as transformation, purification, sharing, permeates our lives.

Water flows through our memories…

Each person goes to the water one by one and blesses themselves.

Pulled three ways – by earth, the moon and the sun – the tides wax and wane day by day, month by month, season by season, beating out the dance of the planet, satellite and star…

Our lives are made possible by the hydrologic cycle…

The miraculous process whereby salty water is transformed into fresh water by evaporation and is redistributed around the planet…

Water ~ North ~ Summer ~ Love

After millions of years, fresh water covered most of the earth...

Like air, water is essential to our survival...

The average human being is roughly 60% water by weight, nearly 40 litres of it carried in trillions of cells...

Water seeps through our skin, escapes from our lungs as vapour and exits every opening of the body...

Human beings have an absolute need for fresh water...

Each person now dips their hands in the water and blesses the four corners of earth.

Water defies human boundaries and human ownership...

Together with the sun, the oceans drive the planet's climate...

Water is the tide of life itself, the sacred source...

As air is a sacred gas, so is water a sacred liquid that links us to all the oceans of the world and ties us back in time to the very birthplace of life...

Leader: Listening to these phrases will likely warm you up to memories of water; times when you have been in water; drunk water to quench your thirst; watched the ocean waves; walked around a lake and been grateful for water.

Contemplative Listening Circle: *Each person now shares a brief water memory; at the end of each sharing, there is a pause. There is no discussion; or debate – this is silent appreciative listening to each one and the phrase:*

Water is the tide of life itself, the sacred source...

is said after each person tells their story.

Leader: Blessed be water essential to our survival.
All: Blessed be water.

Leader: Blessed be water the tide of life itself, the sacred source.
All: Blessed be water.

Leader: Blessed be the water that is carried in our cells.
All: Blessed be water.

Conclude with one minute of contemplative silence.

Water ~ North ~ Summer ~ Love

INVOKING THE FOUR ELEMENTS

"When it comes to living the Christian life, what pope, patriarch, and numerous other religious leaders are urgently teaching is the need for people to change their ways. The traditional term for such a change is conversion… we need a deep spiritual conversion to Earth. (Elizabeth Johnson 2014: 257-258)

Song: *E Tu Kahikatea* One Earth Chants Circle of Friends streaming in Apple Music and Spotify.

This ritual is best done outside and by yourself. You will need this book.

Begin with three minutes of contemplative silence followed by Acknowledgment of Country.

Listen to the song suggested. The English words are:

Stand like the kahikatea (tree); to brave the storms; Embrace and receive we are one together.

Invoke the Elements: Face the north, the direction of heat and warmth and the season of summer. Call in the energy of the north to sustain you for this day. Call in a blessing from this direction. The gift of the north is love. The Spirit of Love flowing through you teaches the power of touching the earth.

Place your hands on your heart for a few moments before you turn.

Face the east, the direction where earth turns toward the light, and the season of spring. Call in the energy of the east to open up new beginnings and new life. Call in a blessing from this direction. The gift of the east is truth. The Spirit of Truth teaches clear seeing.

Place your hands on your eyes for the gift of clear seeing before you turn.

Face the south, the direction of cold and the season of winter. Call in the energy of winter, the place of deep silence. Call in a blessing from this direction. The gift of the south is fortitude. The Spirit of Fortitude teaches the power of strength in adversity.

Clench your hands into a fist, feeling your strength for a few moments before you turn.

Face the west, the direction of falling leaves. Call in the energy of the place where earth turns from the light. Call in a blessing from this direction. The gift of the west is beauty. The Spirit of Beauty surrounds us at all times.

Place your hands in an outward grateful gesture for a few moments and come to stillness.

Conclude with one minute of contemplative silence.

Water ~ North ~ Summer ~ Love

FALLING IN LOVE WITH EARTH

"Ecological Conversion means falling in love with earth as an inherently valuable, living community in which we participate, and bending every effort to be creatively faithful to its well-being, in tune with the living God who brought it into being and cherishes it with unconditional love." **(Elizabeth Johnson 2014: 259)**

https://youtu.be/nwnZphXwTRU this is a YouTube Link to *Falling in Love with Earth* by Mary Tinney RSM.

Begin with three minutes of contemplative silence and Acknowledgment of Country.

Watch *Falling in Love with Earth* and go outside into a quiet peaceful place where you can meditate on the message of the YouTube.

(To *fall in love with earth,* time, contemplation and action are important. Absorbing the beauty of one tree, one plant or one glass of water can be a "simple daily gesture" repeated time and time again.)

Awakening Prayer (*Stand by a plant or tree and gaze contemplatively.*)

In the stillness and presence of Great Spirit, I give thanks for earth and all her generous gifts. I awaken myself to relate emotionally with each tree, each plant and each bird. I intend to do everything in my power to tend to the well-being of earth. Amen.

Mindfulness Prayer (*Stand by a tree and recognise the lungs of earth.*)

Fresh air is the breath in me; flowing through the universe today; breathing consciously with air I am warmed to light and love. Coming home into myself compassionately, I choose to walk reverently in earth, grateful for my natural gifts. Amen.

Consciousness Prayer (*Walk with deliberation and consciousness.*)

My consciousness is deepened, every step I take in earth, grounding me with reverence for the whole community. Amen.

Gratefulness Prayer (*Return to the seat outside where you began this meditation.*)

I give thanks for all that is in this Earth Community; aware of Sacred Presence gifts of the universe now beyond my imagining. Amen.

In the stillness and presence of Great Spirit, I give thanks for the elements that sustain me – fire, water, air and earth. Amen.

Conclude with one minute of contemplative silence.

NEW STORY IN SONG

"It is worth noting that… throughout the past few centuries, spiritual behaviour, especially spiritual 'progress' often was judged in terms of linear time…Today, the emphasis tends to be on the quality of the experience rather than the duration of the exercise. And we give significantly more time to spatial factors, such as the ambience of prayer, places and times, body posture in prayer, environmental context, and group support structure." **(Diarmuid O'Murchu 2003:116)**

https://youtu.be/DtyDxjwd7oU This is a You Tube link to Connie Barlow's version of Silent Night for the cosmically inclined. (Used with permission)

Gather in a circle in the dark and have the YouTube ready to use on the data projector.

Begin with three minutes of contemplative silence and Acknowledgment of Country.

Watch the YouTube together.

Sing together

Silent night. Holy night. All is calm. All is bright.
Life abounds upon Earth. Life abounds upon Earth.

1. PLAN-ets GRACE-ful-ly CIR-cle the SUN
STAR-dust CY-cles through EV-er-y ONE

2. RA-di-ant BEAMS from PRI-mor-dial STARS
CLUMPED in-to PLAN-ets like VE-nus and MARS

3. CAR-bon NI-tro-gen AND cal-ci-UM
ALL were BORN in-side AN-ces-tral SUNS

4. DEATH and re-CY-cling of MILL-ions of STARS
BROUGHT forth PLAN-ets and ALL that we ARE

5. SIL-ver GOLD and TI-ta-ni-UM
FORGED in STARS be-fore EARTH had be-GUN

6. FLAR-ing FORTH a-cross HEAV-en a-BOVE
SU-per-NO-vas made ALL that we LOVE

Silent night. Holy night. All is calm. All is bright.
Life abounds upon Earth. Life abounds upon Earth.

Conclude with one minute of contemplative silence.

Water ~ North ~ Summer ~ Love

LITANY OF GRIEF

"The word 'water' is cited forty-seven times in Pope Francis' encyclical, Laudato Si'. This demonstrates the great value and concern Pope Francis places on water as a sacred and essential part of life." Maryknoll Office for Global Concerns https://maryknollogc.org/article/laudato-si-and-water

Background: Pope Francis identifies five key problems related to water:

1. The lack of access to clean drinking water "indispensable for human life and for supporting terrestrial and aquatic ecosystems" [28];
2. The challenges for food production due to droughts and disparities in water availability and "water poverty" [28];
3. The continued prevalence of water-related diseases afflicting the poor [29];
4. The contamination of groundwater [29];
5. The trend toward privatisation and commodification of a resource to which the pope describes access to as a "basic and universal human right" [30].

This ritual is a meditative reflection on a growing global concern, outlined by Pope Francis in Laudato Si', which is the lack of appreciation for water as sacred.

Begin with three minutes of contemplative silence and Acknowledgment of Country.

Litany: I grieve today for the pollution in our oceans.

> I am part of earth, air, fire and water; and earth, air, fire and water are part of me; I lament any forgetfulness on my part.

I grieve today for the contamination of ground water.

> I am part of earth, air, fire and water; and earth, air, fire and water are part of me; I lament any forgetfulness on my part.

I grieve today for those without fresh water.

> I am part of earth, air, fire and water; and earth, air, fire and water are part of me; I lament any forgetfulness on my part.

I grieve today for underwater species affected by plastic in the oceans.

> I am part of earth, air, fire and water; and earth, air, fire and water are part of me; I lament any forgetfulness on my part.

As with all death and dying, we grieve the loss, the presence and the relationship. Today we grieve.

Conclude with one minute of contemplative silence.

Water ~ North ~ Summer ~ Love

EVOLVING UNIVERSE

"So Christian discipleship today is evolving… into a collaborative endeavour for empowering love and justice… with the historical Jesus as the exemplary disciple and all others called into discipleship in their enterprise… it is a global enterprise embracing all that is holy and sacred within the entire web of life, cosmic and planetary alike." (Diarmuid O'Murchu 2017:35)

Song: *Could it Be* –streaming on Apple Music and Spotify

Begin with three minutes of contemplative silence followed by Acknowledgment of Country. Take a copy of this book out into the garden and play the song *Could it be*?

> Could it be? Could it be? Could it be that the Universe could see?
> Could it be that it is self-aware?
> Could it be you and me are the consciousness of the Universe?
>
> Could it be? Could it be that this consciousness comes from Mystery?
> From the Source of all Life and all things?
> Could it be you and me are the consciousness of mystery?
>
> Could it be? Could it be that Mystery's the Ground of all Being?
> Energy pulsing with Sacred Power?
> Could it be you and me are the consciousness of the Ground of Being?
> *2006 by Jan Novotka's Music, LLC (ASCAP). All rights reserved.*

Reflective Quotes for Pondering
"We need to redefine human rights in the light of our ecological vision. We need a means of recognising and protecting the roles of other than human members of Earth Community." (Thomas Berry 1990)

"Creation is happening as we speak and we are evolving – nothing ever stays stagnant including the cells of our bodies – they are always in the process of change – we see evolution in the cycle of the butterfly; we see evolution in the cycle of the tomato seed; we all know that we are evolving and so is everything that is part of all that is." (Margie Abbott 2018 presentation World Day of Prayer)

Reflective Meditative Gazing: When you pass a tree, you can greet the tree with "You are my sister" – pause and gaze around at the clouds, sky, and growing things and internally say "I am part of you and you are part of me as we evolve and grow." When you gaze around at the birds and insects, you can greet them "We are evolving and are part of Earth Community".
Conclude with one minute of contemplative silence.

Water ~ North ~ Summer ~ Love

HEART ATTUNEMENT WITH ALL THAT IS

"The first and most essential element in an ecological conversion is coming to an effective awareness and acceptance that everything in our world is connected… Ecologists call this network the 'web of life' which includes animals, plants and everything which can be understood to be alive. They also speak of 'the web of the cosmos', which includes the non-living arts of our universe, ranging from the most distant galaxies to the most microscopic elements." (Donal Dorr 2017: 161)

Dr Gillian Ross has a Heart Meditation http://drgillianross.com/shop/meditation/ $15
(There are two other meditations on Breath and Light on the same CD.)
This ritual is inspired by Margaret Bullitt-Jonas https://revivingcreation.org
Begin with three minutes of contemplative silence and Acknowledgment of Country.

Prepare for the meditation by placing your left hand over your heart and close your eyes. Listen to your heartbeat as you breathe in and out in the silence. (Allow one to two minutes.) Now, please place your right hand over your left hand and put your thumbs together and place the soles of your feet on the floor. We are connected to earth and conscious of our heart beating.

Open your eyes and slowly prepare for the meditation by praying this prayer of St Francis (adapted)

> I choose to be a channel of peace; where there is hatred I choose love;
> Where there is injury I choose forgiveness; where there is self-doubt I choose faith;
> Where there is despair in life I choose hope; where there is darkness I choose light.
>
> I attune my heart to waking up; noticing; taking responsibility; mindfulness and stillness. I am in touch with my awakening heart.
>
> I attune my heart to all beings and all species who are suffering; I am in touch with my suffering heart.
>
> I attune my heart to action, transformation and social justice. I am in touch with my radiant heart.
>
> For Great Spirit flowing through my heart I am grateful.

Now listen to the *Heart Meditation* by Dr Gillian Ross.

This is best done sitting in a quiet place outside where you will not be disturbed.

Conclude with one minute of contemplative silence.

RIVER SUNDAY: WORLD RIVERS DAY (4TH SUNDAY IN SEPTEMBER)

"The environment is part of the logic of receptivity. It is on loan to each generation, which must then hand it on to the next." Portuguese Bishop's Conference 2003:159
"The ego driven madness of our current market economy, blinded to the finiteness of resources, must be called to account before our planet burns up or sinks into the ocean depths." (Nellie McLaughlin RSM 2015:34)

(Adapted with permission www. normanhabel.com/)

A collection of images of rivers in Australia and other countries can be placed in the setting where this ritual is to take place.

Begin with three minutes of contemplative silence and Acknowledgment of Country.

Welcome!

Read the words of this song by Norm Habel ©

Be still and feel the presence of God, the presence pulsing, pulsing through Earth. Be still and feel the pulse of God. Be still and hear the Spirit of God, the Spirit breathing, breathing through Earth. Be still and hear the breath of God. Be still; behold the glory of God, the glory filling, filling this Earth. Be still, behold the face of God.

Leader: In the name of the Spirit of God
who hovered over the primal waters.
In the name of the Word of God
who parted the waters for Earth to appear.
In the name of the Wisdom of God,
who filled the deep with amazing design! Amen.
All: Holy! Holy! Holy!
The rivers are filled with God's presence.

Lament

Leader: Your Spirit is the life impulse in all things, renewing the barren and healing the wounded, groaning in anticipation of a new creation, stirring a new life born of water and the Spirit.

All: We lament! We are sorry. We have polluted our rivers with poisons. We have treated our streams as waste dumps. We have turned living waters into death-traps. We have wasted precious waters in luxury living.

Water ~ North ~ Summer ~ Love

All: Thank you, Great Spirit for the rivers,

living waters that are part of our life on Earth.

Reading: Psalm 104:27–33 'God's sustenance of Earth' – the psalm writer celebrates how God sustains all life on Earth through the Spirit and calls on God to rejoice in God's own creation.

Leader: We call to mind all the rivers of Australia especially the Murray, the Darling and all the streams that flow to the sea.

All: We invite the country creeks to sing.

Leader: Perch, eel and platypus, trout streams and gleaming fountains.

All: We invite the fauna to praise God with us.

Leader: Ibis, heron and mountain duck, dragonflies and sleepy tortoises.

All: We join with the waters in praising God.

Leader: Waterfalls singing upstream and waves dancing at the river mouth.

All: We celebrate the song of the river!

Leader: "Earth is full of your creatures; yonder is the sea, great and wide, creeping things innumerable are there; living things both small and great." Psalm 104: 24-26

Creed: We believe Earth is a sanctuary,
a sacred planet filled with God's presence,
a home for us to share with our kin.
We believe that God became flesh and blood,
became a part of Earth,
a human being called Jesus Christ,
who lived and breathed and spoke among us.
We believe that the risen Jesus
is the Christ at the core of creation
reconciling all things to God,
renewing all creation and filling the universe.
We believe the Spirit renews life in creation
groans in empathy with a suffering creation,
and waits with us for the rebirth of creation.
We believe that with Christ we will rise
and with Christ we will celebrate a new creation.

Conclude with one minute of contemplative silence.

Water ~ North ~ Summer ~ Love

UNIVERSE IS SACRED

"The foundation of Ecozoic activism is, of course, the Great story – the epic of evolution. The Great story is everybody's story; it is the overarching story of everything and all times. Crucially, it's a creation story still in process. The Great story thus embraces our visions for the future as well as the scientifically familiar record of the past... Ecozoic activism will manifest in forms as diverse as any other expression of the life force. Yet beneath the diversity of *doing* will reside a shared core of *being*... to distinguish and nurture such core ways of being, such attitudes of the heart, is thus crucial to the emerging Ecozoic Era.' (Michael Dowd and Connie Barlow 2001:14)

https://youtu.be/On7ma4UFVVM This YouTube link will take you to a three minute contemplative meditation by Ronda La Rue and David Whyte. (Used with permission)

Begin with three minutes of contemplative silence and Acknowledgment of Country.

If possible, pray this ritual outside.

After you watch the YouTube, take a few moments to walk around the space that you are in and become aware of light; of nature; of air; of clouds; of anything growing; of pebbles; stones or small weeds.

Sit in stillness.

Play the YouTube again and take a few moments to sit in stillness and, with your hands on your heart, open yourself up to the interior places within where inspiration, creativity, will power and graces abound.

> Blessed be earth.
> Blessed be the sky at night.
> Blessed be all the birds departing on their long journeys.
> Blessed be the 'garden of creativity' growing in me
> Blessed be the leaves in the wind.
> Blessed be the evening ocean.
> Blessed be the outback and ancient bushland.
> Blessed be the tendrils of plants and grasses.
> Blessed be all living and non-living members of Earth Community.

Conclude with one minute of contemplative silence.

ELEMENT: FIRE

DIRECTION: WEST

SEASON: AUTUMN

GIFT: BEAUTY

Fire ~ West ~ Autumn ~ Beauty

RECONCILIATION

"**National Reconciliation Week is a time for all Australians to learn about our shared histories, cultures, and achievements, and to explore how each of us can contribute to achieving reconciliation in Australia.' (Reconciliation Australia Website)**

This Reconciliation ritual may be used throughout the year, on National Sorry Day or during National Reconciliation Week.

Background: Reconciliation is an everyday challenge. In 1998, Australia stopped to recognise for the first time a National Sorry Day – 26th May.

Sorry Day precedes National Reconciliation Week, which commences on 27th May (the anniversary of the 1967 referendum) and concludes on 3rd June (the anniversary of the 1992 Mabo judgment).

Song: *Marrandil* Gurrumul streaming on Apple Music and Spotify.

Begin outside with your shoes off and your feet on earth. Begin with a minute of silence and gaze around you and take a couple of deep breaths. Listen to Gurrumul.

Acknowledge the Elders of the Aboriginal and Torres Strait Islanders living, dead and emerging. Warm up respectfully and contemplatively. Honour their presence on this land for thousands and thousands of years before white settlement.

Close your eyes and repeat internally "Sacred Land I acknowledge and lament!"

Acknowledge sorrow for the invasion of land, with no treaty.

Close your eyes and repeat internally "Sacred Land I acknowledge and lament!"

Acknowledge that European ancestors stripped many of the creative ways the First Nations People cared for land, and as a result productivity and vitality was greatly diminished.

Close your eyes and repeat internally "Sacred Land I acknowledge and lament!"

Acknowledge sorrow for the actions that have robbed Indigenous Australia of life, culture, law and language.

Close your eyes and repeat internally "Sacred Land I acknowledge and lament!"

Acknowledge that many First Australians were massacred or destroyed violently.

Close your eyes and repeat internally "Sacred Land I acknowledge and lament!"

Conclude the ritual by listening to Gurrumul and then take a handful of soil and let it run through your fingers. Conclude with a minute of contemplative silence.

Fire ~ West ~ Autumn ~ Beauty

A MEDITATION ON LOVE

"**Let us sing as we go. May our struggles and our concern for this planet never take away the joy of our hope. (LS: 244)**

Song: *Ubi Caritas* Katie Ketchum – streaming Apple Music and Spotify.

Begin with three minutes of contemplative silence followed by Acknowledgment of Country.

Sound the Tibetan bells (or download Centring Prayer App for free which has bell tones and timers). Listen to Ubi Caritas. "Where Love Is".

Light a candle.

Open your eyes and focus on the votive candle and allow the flickering of the flame and the centre of the wick to call you to a deep awareness of the unconditional love that flows through you.

Be still in the knowledge that you are deeply loved. Sourced and sustained, your attention is riveted.

Ponder on these words by Veronica Lawson RSM "Thinking cosmically elicits wonder and respect for all beings and especially for God who is Source and Sustainer of all." (Lawson 2015:72)

Read this poem by Elizabeth Young RSM (used with permission) and experience waves of love permeating all that lives in our Earth Community.

Morning walk

>It quietly invites all those who peer –
>amidst tall green grass, a trembling cobweb sheer
>and every water drop a diamond or tear –
>this beauty cries.
>
>And in ordinary, delicate grace –
>the bright jewellery droplet and spider's lace –
>God's sweet, mysterious love right here in this place,
>then glory is raised.
>
>Oh, what a truly precious gift to live
>when life ebbs from so many, as through a sieve
>and hearts are wrung, and there is nothing left to give,
>yet hope survives.

Conclude with one minute of contemplative silence.

Fire ~ West ~ Autumn ~ Beauty

THE FIRE

"**Or are we like a flame, said several early systems thinkers. As a flame keeps its shape by transforming the stuff it burns, so does the open system. As the open system consumes the matter that passes through it, so does it also process information – ever breaking down and building up, renewed. Like fire, a system both transforms and is transformed by that on which it feeds.**" (Joanna Macy, Molly Young Brown 2014:41)

Song: *Sacred Fire* Kathy Sherman – streaming on Apple Music and Spotify.

Begin with three minutes of contemplative silence followed by Acknowledgment of Country.

Listen to the song and then do deep breaths as you settle and become present to this moment.

Sufi Fire Breath: Relax, breathing your natural breath. As you do the breath for the fire element, attune your heartbeat and, and experience the energy pulsing through your body.

Inhale through the mouth and exhale through the nose.

Repeat this Fire Breath five times.

Leader: Today we will adapt *Lectio Divina* to reflect on this poem by Trevor Parton (used with permission) and as we gather in this circle let us listen to a reading of the poem.

"*Lectio Divina...* is an ancient practice and can include any sacred text – a passage that moves you, a poem you love, or an image that is calling for your attention." (Christine Valters Paintner 2011:18)

The Fire

>I gazed into the fire
>And wondered
>What is the energy
>Coursing through the veins of history
>Like blood
>And bathing me with warmth?
>This is its last gasp,
>For heat is the end of the energy line;
>Entropy, disorder, wave's end, dissipation.
>And what did this energy do
>After its journey from the sun?
>It warmed earth around the seed,

Made sugar in the leaves,
Wood in the stems and trunks
Until the tree stood up and said
"I am, I am"
A tree that is, and carbon, oxygen and
Sunlight too, and bits of you.
And I am supernova too, and galaxy,
And whatever came before that
I am, I am, I am, I am………………..

Leader: Let us listen to the poem being read again and this time you will be invited to share one word that stays with you.

Circle sharing with pauses to allow slowing down, becoming fully present, and maintaining a sense of awe and wonder as each one speaks.

Leader: Let us listen to the poem for a third time and you are asked to listen for an invitation that stays with you.

Circle sharing with pauses to allow slowing down, becoming fully present, and maintaining a sense of awe and wonder as each one speaks.

Group Sharing: In groups of three, share favourite images and metaphors from this poem and what you are being invited to allow emergence in your own life.

Reflection:	"I gazed into the fire."
All:	I gazed into the fire.
Leader:	I gazed into
All:	I gazed into
Leader:	I gazed
All:	I gazed

Conclude with one minute of contemplative silence.

Fire ~ West ~ Autumn ~ Beauty

IGNITING SPARKS:
GREETING THE DAWN

"A renewed experience of natural symbols of water, earth, fire and wind and life forms can serve as a salutary antidote to the excessive analysis, rationalisation and fragmentation of our mechanically oriented world." (Sean McDonagh 1986:95)

Resources: You will need cotton wool soaked in methylated spirits in a safe, fire-proof container such as a wok, or sand soaked in methylated spirits in a pottery bowl. Remember to place it on a brick or something that can withstand heat.

Setting the Space: Place the wok with cloths surrounding it. An unlit candle is placed in the setting. Invite people to gather around the focus in a circle. This is an outside ritual in the dark. Begin with three minutes of contemplative silence followed by Acknowledgment of Country.

Song: *Sacred Fire* Jan Novotka – streaming Apple Music and Spotify

Sacred Presence Fire Within, loving and living within us, from the Source of all that is; Fire is living morning praise; the dawn proclaims light and love.

As the wok is lit, *Sacred Fire* is played.

> Sacred Fire, burning before me;
> burning within me; deep in my soul!
> Sacred Fire, transforming Fire,
> recreate me. Make me whole.

> © 1994 by Jan Novotka's Music, LLC (ASCAP). All rights reserved.

Leader: From sparks fire is created. As we focus on the burning fire, let us meditate for a few moments on some of the ways that we experience Divine Sparks in our lives.

Blessing: The presence of Sacred Spirit is with us.

As we go forth into today, we open our eyes mindfully to the 'spark' of Divine Presence around us in the people we meet, the non-human we meet and the places we go. Amen.

Sing the chant *Sacred Fire*

> Sacred Fire, burning before me;
> burning within me; deep in my soul!
> Sacred Fire, transforming Fire,
> recreate me. Make me whole.

Conclude with one minute of contemplative silence.

Fire ~ West ~ Autumn ~ Beauty

COMMUNITY EARTH RITUAL: AUTUMN EQUINOX

"Autumn Equinox is the point of balance of light and dark in the dark part of the cycle. Sun is equidistant between North and South… Autumn Equinox is a time of thanksgiving for the harvest – for its empowerment and nourishment, and it is also a time of leave-taking and sorrow, as life declines. (Glenys Livingstone 2005:301)

This is a link to Glenys Livingstone's website and there you can purchase the autumn meditation https://pagaian.org/pagaian-prayers-invoking-her/

A Possible Process for Creating a Ritual – Remote Preparation

For several years, a community group has been meeting to celebrate the Autumn Equinox and create a ritual together.

Two weeks before the scheduled ritual, an email is sent to the group to remind them to reflect on autumn and allow their contemplative stance to flow freely.

"For those of you who are coming for the first time we have been working with the idea of a 'contemplative stance' – allowing anything that emerges in us as autumn nears - thought; idea; action; musing; daydreaming; synchronicity etc. so make a note and bring something to celebrate this at the autumn equinox ritual.

We will celebrate with whatever you bring to contribute to the ritual – out of your reflections since the last ritual – poetry; music; sacred space décor; symbols; readings; movement; drama; dance; and art works."

Suggested Process for Creating Ritual on the Day

Gather in a circle and acknowledge the land and original ancestors.

Begin with three minutes of contemplative silence.

The leader invites each person one by one to share what they have brought to the ritual.

The listening process is discerning and appreciative.

Using contemplative listening (one person speaks at a time and whatever is suggested is accepted without interruption or disagreement), the group then suggests possible placing and timing of the texts, décor, music, dance, etc. This usually works out smoothly and with great respect for the gifts shared among the group.

The ritual is enacted.

Conclude with one minute of contemplative silence.

Fire ~ West ~ Autumn ~ Beauty

BUSHFIRE SUNDAY

In 2015, scientist Peter Stott at the UK's Met Office said that a study on climate change was an important step in attribution science. "What has been lacking up to now is a robust calculation of how much more likely extreme temperatures and rainfall have become worldwide." (*The Guardian* April 2015)

(Adapted with permission www.normanhabel.com/)

Gather gum leaves for this ritual. Burn some beforehand so that half of them are blackened. Place in a bowl in the gathering setting.

Begin with three minutes of contemplative silence and Acknowledgment of Country.

Leader: In Australia and across the world there are many more bushfires reported. We gather in compassion for all the pain and loss that bushfires cause for humans and non-humans. We can think of the extremes of climate change as Stations of Unnecessary Sorrow! We can lament the loss in the adapted words of Norm Habel.

All: We respect the North Wind but when that wind whips up flames into a hurricane of fire, we weep and wonder why.

Silence

All: We respect eucalyptus trees but when eucalyptus trees fuel swirling balls of fire that land on houses miles and miles away, we weep and wonder why.

Silence

All: We respect bushland creatures, but when scorched birds from the sky and koalas are reduced to cinders, we weep and wonder why.

Silence

All: We call on forest families to celebrate: but when homes and habitat are reduced to ashes and children die, we weep and wonder why.

Let us pray together: Compassionate Great Spirit, calling us to consciousness to walk reverently on earth stirred by your Divine Presence, we give thanks for all that is, in reverent gratitude. Amen.

Leader: Take a moment to crush the blackened leaves in your hands to release the scent of oil, and remember with compassion the suffering and loss of so many.

Conclude with one minute of contemplative silence.

Fire ~ West ~ Autumn ~ Beauty

ROUND TABLES JUSTICE REFLECTION RITUAL

"When you are confronted by evidence that the faith in which you were brought up no longer provides an adequate explanation for the nature, meaning and purpose of your life, you have three choices. You can refuse to accept the evidence and continue as before. You can abandon the faith you grew with because it has proved to be inadequate. Or, third, you can accept the new knowledge and use it to develop a more mature understanding of what lies at the core of your beliefs… his requires courage and a plethora of other virtues that have been gathering dust in your spirit." (John Feehan 2012:148)

Round Tables Helen Kearins RSM streaming Apple Music and Spotify

This ritual is best done as a walking meditation, speaking aloud the words of *Round Tables* as you go. You will need this book outside.

Begin with three minutes of contemplative silence and Acknowledgment of Country.

"Been a long, long journey and my heart is yearning and I won't settle until I've found somewhere I find meaning, equal ways of being where the power is shared all around so I seek…

Round tables where we are all able to sit and share our good wine; talk our hearts' deep longing, see our words shape song in clear voices creating new rhyme.

No top or bottom, let it not be forgotten, everyone has equality here. No lines and angles, something more like a bangle, and the end and beginning aren't clear when we're at…

Round tables where we are all able to sit and share our good wine; talk our hearts' deep longing, see our words shape song in clear voices creating new rhyme.

Walk in mother, you can come to brother, there is room for everyone here, take your place beside us, let no-one divide us as the circle melts away fear. When we're at…

Round tables where we are all able to sit and share our good wine; talk our hearts' deep longing, see our words shape song in clear voices creating new rhyme.

I can fight just causes even wild, wild horses cannot keep me from standing my ground, but I need sustaining and there's scant remaining in the church of the emptying sound. So we'll build…

Round tables where we are all able to sit and share our good wine; talk our hearts' deep longing, see our words shape song in clear voices creating new rhyme.

I will sit beside you, but I will not hide you from the pain that engagement may bring. I will meet your gaze and we'll create new ways for our truth and our passion to ring! We'll create…

Round tables where we are all able to sit and share our good wine; talk our hearts' deep longing, see our words shape song in clear voices creating new rhyme."

(Used with permission Helen Kearins rsm)

At a later time, you may decide to create a mandala using some of these images.

Conclude your walk with some deep breaths and one minute of contemplative silence.

Fire ~ West ~ Autumn ~ Beauty

WALKING FOR HOPE

"Active hope is a practice. Like t'chai and gardening. It is something we do rather than have. It is a process we can apply to any situation, and it involves three key steps. First, we take a clear view of reality; second, we identify what we hope for, in terms of the direction we'd like things to move in or values we'd like to see expressed; and third, we take steps to move ourselves or our situation in that direction." (Chris Johnstone March April 2014 in *Resurgence Ecologist*)

Song: *Unlock Your Memory* Murray Kyle https://murraykyle.bandcamp.com/track/unlock-your-memory

Begin with three minutes of contemplative silence and Acknowledgment of Country.

Take this book outside with you.

Read this excerpt from the Environmental Sabbath Invitation in 1989.

"We who have lost our sense and our senses – our touch, our smell, our vision of who we are, we who frantically force and press all things, without rest for body or Spirit, hurting our earth and injuring ourselves; we call a halt. We want to rest. We need to rest and allow the earth to rest. We need to reflect and to rediscover the mystery that lives in us, that is the ground of every unique expression of life, the source of the fascination that calls all things to communion. We declare a Sabbath, a space of quiet; for simply being and for recovering the forgotten truths; for learning how to live again."

Choose a walking track where you can feel fresh air; warmth of the sun; see many examples of shrubs, trees and flowers, and hear the birdsong.

Pause and bow to one of the trees and say "Namaste" – I honour the Divine in you.

Then read: From Mary Southard (Art Blog 'To our fellow earthlings', 9 May 2019; **used with permission**)

"For quite some time now, we have been hearing statements that refer to this era as a time of terrible upheaval and chaos, a time of *impossible questions*. We know the list: global warming, polar ice caps and glaciers melting, the sixth great extinction of species in Earth's 4.5 billion year history, increasing political instability and violence, migrations of the desperate."

The scope of this dilemma and its consequences are terrifying, but what can I do? How am I to process this conundrum? I've been awakened from my cultural haze, now aware of my addictions so deeply rooted in an ingrained illusion of separateness. I've been awakened to the truth of what it means to live in a world where all is intimately interconnected. And as a result, I'm compelled to take a quantum leap from awareness into action.

We can no longer consider ourselves as separate from each other, especially those who are not like us. And we can no longer act as if we are separate from the natural world: the waters, the air, the soil. A major transformation is required of us. Awaken we must!"

Continue walking, listening to Murray Kyle's song "Unlock your Memory"

Fire ~ West ~ Autumn ~ Beauty

Pause and read: From Mary Southard (Art Blog 'To our fellow earthlings', 9 May 2019; **used with permission)**

"Let us make the journey back home, back into Earth saturated with Divinity! Let it be a journey of the heart where we acknowledge to our beautiful and generous planet that we have been distant, blind, and perhaps frightened to think about this. Let us once again become intimate and tender with trees, and grasses and soil; with atmosphere, flowers, plants, animals, insects. Let us drink of their beauty and wisdom. Let us go there now, and promise ourselves ample time outdoors each day this month so we can breathe, see, feel, explore, and recognise our Oneness with the natural world. Let Earth nourish our wounded human souls as we pray and act to heal her. And let us practise gratitude to those Earthlings who daily nourish our bodies as food, drink, clothing, and shelter; and who delight our souls with their beauty and mystery. Above all, let us fall in love again with our Earth and allow ourselves to be filled with her wonder and magnificence, to be filled with the Divinity of this vibrant community of life in which we are embedded!"

Continue walking and listen again to "Unlock Your Memory".

Pause for a reflection

Sit or stand near one of the trees, shrubs or flowers. Slowly let yourself drop into the following words, taking plenty of time to pause.

"Let us fall in love again with Earth and allow ourselves to be filled with her wonder and magnificence, to be filled with the Divinity of this vibrant community of life in which we are embedded." (Mary Southard)

Wisdom is your breath in me; guiding, leading me into breaking fresh ground generously.

Treading consciously in earth; leading me to step with care; coming home into myself I walk reverently in earth.

Continue walking for five to ten minutes and then pause and…

Read this excerpt from the Environmental Sabbath Invitation in 1989.

"We who have lost our sense and our senses – our touch, our smell, our vision of who we are, we who frantically force and press all things, without rest for body or Spirit, hurting our earth and injuring ourselves; we call a halt. We want to rest. We need to rest and allow the earth to rest. We need to reflect and to rediscover the mystery that lives in us, that is the ground of every unique expression of life, the source of the fascination that calls all things to communion. We declare a Sabbath, a space of quiet; for simply being and for recovering the forgotten truths; for learning how to live again."

Interior resolve:

I pledge to rest, wait, and be for ten minutes each day.

I pledge to download an app called *Daily Calm* to assist me.

I pledge to honour all around me as sacred.

Conclude with one minute of contemplative silence.

Fire ~ West ~ Autumn ~ Beauty

JESUS BY THE FIRE

"Jesus provides a good role model for mental wellbeing, not just that he regularly took time out for himself to go up to the mountain to pray… he was big on relationships… he was big on sharing meals with his disciples." (Dave Jorna *Australian Catholics* Winter 2019:15)

Meditation: Human like Us. (This response by Michael Morwood is used with permission.)

Begin with three minutes of contemplative silence and Acknowledgment of Country.

(Sit in a solitary place outside and reflect on these words praying them slowly and mindfully.)

Jesus, human like us you met with friends and ate cooked fish.

You felt the warmth of the fire, smelt the smoke, human like us.

Jesus, human like us you waited for the catch of the day.

You felt the warmth of the fire, smelt the smoke, human like us.

Jesus, having caught fish at your command, your friend arrives on the shore and you offer to cook breakfast with bread and fish.

You felt the warmth of the fire, smelt the smoke, human like us.

Jesus, you ate with friends and strangers alike.

You felt the warmth of the fire, smelt the smoke, human like us.

When they had finished breakfast, Jesus said to Simon Peter, "Simon son of John, do you love me more than these?"

You felt the warmth of the fire and invited a response of love.

Jesus, you invite us to expand our ideas about you as a prophet of justice.

You felt the warmth of the fire and invited a response of love.

Jesus, you open our minds to the power of love.

You felt the warmth of the fire and invited a response of love.

Jesus, you open our mind to a 'Companionship of Empowerment'.

You felt the warmth of the fire and invited a response of love.

To conclude this reflection: A journal idea – Which of the statements touched your own experience most deeply? Which of them felt as if it were calling you to awaken your consciousness?

Conclude with one minute of contemplative silence.

Fire ~ West ~ Autumn ~ Beauty

MINDFULNESS IN AUTUMN

"You might well ask: Then how are we to practice mindfulness? My answer is: keep your attention focussed on the work, be alert and ready to handle ably and intelligently any situation which may arise-this is mindfulness." (Thich Nhat Hanh 1975:14)

Gather some autumn leaves and place them in a circle at your feet, outside in the open air. Take this book with you.

Begin with three minutes of contemplative silence and Acknowledgment of Country.

Pick up one of the autumn leaves and notice the veins, the lines and the shape and texture.

Close your eyes and do the Sufi fire breath five times. Inhale through your mouth and exhale through your nose.

Place the leaves mindfully back into the circle of leaves.

A way to help us dwell in the present moment is to practise answering this question over and over "What is present?"

As you look around, notice what is present and answer the question a few times "What is present?"

The gift of autumn is beauty.

Notice the beauty around you and smell what is present. Savour the smell and inhale the perfume within.

Notice the beauty around you and touch what is present. Feel the shape and texture and leave your hand there for a moment. Be mindful of the texture under your hand.

Notice the beauty around you and hear what is present. Close your eyes and listen to the sounds and then open your eyes and breathe in and out with gratitude.

Notice the beauty around you and taste what is present. This may be metaphorical, depending on where you are. Lick your lips and taste.

Notice the beauty around you and see what is present. Gaze contemplatively and with mindfulness.

By the autumn leaves breathe in and breathe out with thankfulness for the life of these leaves now spent.

Blessing

I bless my forehead and open my eyes to behold this silence and beauty.

I bless my hands and strengthen my resolve to act justly, walk humbly and love deeply.

I bless my ears and listen for the sounds of love in the web of life.

I bless my heart and resolve to act to transform and be transformed.

Conclude with one minute of contemplative silence

Fire ~ West ~ Autumn ~ Beauty

MANTRAS:
AN AUTUMN MEDITATON

"… my sense is that our culture cannot endure without a re-sacralisation of consciousness and a re-enchantment of the world. Rather than steal the spiritualities of ancient peoples, we had better start fossicking around for spiritual ecologies of our own…" **(David Tacey 2016:13)**

Choose an outdoor setting for this contemplative ritual.

Song: *Creative Contemplative* Jan Novotka - streaming Apple Music and Spotify.

Begin with three minutes of contemplative silence and Acknowledgment of Country.

Stand and Face the West: Today I welcome the Season of Autumn. I face the West and draw in a deep breath of fresh air. I invoke a blessing on this time of silent reflection.

Close your eyes: Breathe in the sounds of Earth Community. **Open your eyes:** Breathe out the sounds of autumn.

Close your eyes: Breathe in the smells of Earth Community. **Open your eyes:** Breathe out the smells of autumn.

Close your eyes: Breathe in the sights of Earth Community. **Open your eyes:** Breathe out the sight of autumn.

Close your eyes: Breathe in the taste of Earth Community. **Open your eyes:** Breathe out the taste of autumn.

Close your eyes: Breathe in and allow yourself to be touched by Earth Community**. Open your eyes:** Breathe out and feel the touch of autumn.

Mindfulness Meditation: (*read, pause; and savour…*)

Compassionately, I choose to sit reverently in earth; in this inner stillness now, evolving and unfolding

Consciously; I reverently appreciate all that is now binding me to one and All!

Listen to *Creative Contemplative.*

Creative contemplative am I, moving slowly into the deep. Tasting and touching pearls and pain; in the depths of creation's soul.

Creative contemplative am I, coming home to soil and sea. Fire, air, and sunlight transform me into wholeness, child of Earth.

Creative contemplative am I, living deeply from the Abyss. Creating what's never been. Giving birth to God in our world.

Creative contemplative am I, honouring all life as I live. Blessing the Earth with tenderness; Great Communion, one with what is.

©*2006 by Jan Novotka's Music, LLC (ASCAP). All rights reserved.*

Conclude with one minute of contemplative silence.

CONVERSION AND ACTION NOW: CLIMATE EMERGENCY

"Francis addressed his encyclical as an appeal to 'the whole human family,' requesting 'a new dialogue about how we are shaping the future of our planet,' he called not only for conversation but ultimately conversion and action to better care for a common earthly home that 'is falling into serious disrepair.' And in the case of climate change, address an urgent need to develop policies so that, in the next few years, the emission of carbon dioxide and other highly polluting gases can be drastically reduced." (Brian Roewe, *Earthbeat* NCR 2019)

Song: *Mother Earth* Betsy Rose. Streaming Apple Music and Spotify.

Begin with three minutes of contemplative silence and Acknowledgment of Country.

Listen to *Mother Earth*.

Examen of Consciousness

Where do I stand? What am I yet to learn? Where am I being lead? Am I open to conversion and action?

Read these excerpts from David Suzuki's book *The Sacred Balance,* written in 1996 (used with permission).

Humanity has never before faced such a threat: the collapse of the very elements that keep us alive. (6)

- We join with earth and each other to awaken to this threat.

Every worldview describes a universe in which everything is connected with everything else. Stars, clouds, forest, oceans and human beings are interconnected components of a single system in which nothing can exist in isolation. (12)

- We join with earth and each other to stand for justice.

Philosophers from ancient Greece believed the material universe was divisible into just four elements – air, water, earth and fire. Each human being was compounded of these four elements in varying proportions – air, water, earth and fire interacting to generate and sustain life. (28)

- We join with earth and each other to create practices of gratitude.

Today we believe that life cannot arise spontaneously, that life can only come from life. But once, at the very beginning, the first organism from which we are all descended was sparked into being, full of a life force that has so far persisted tenaciously for close to 4 billion years. (114)

- We join with earth and each other to renew our minds and reinvigorate our hearts.

Take five big breaths – breathe in hope and breathe out despair.

Listen to *Mother Earth*.

Conclude with one minute of contemplative silence.

Fire ~ West ~ Autumn ~ Beauty

INFINITE BEAUTY

"At the end, we will find ourselves face to face with the infinite beauty of God (cf. 1 Corinthians 13:12) and be able to read with admiration and happiness the mystery of the universe." (LS 243)

Begin with three minutes of contemplative silence and Acknowledgment of Country.

Warm up to this meditation on beauty by watching Leonard Cohen singing *Anthem*.

https://youtu.be/mDTph7mer3I

Reflect on what has inspired you lately. Where have you experienced 'cracks' that let the light in? What has challenged you lately? What has excited and thrilled you recently?

Pause.

Reflection:

A Litany of Beauty

>Blessed be Creative Flame in the darkness.
>
>Blessed all who are awake to justice.
>
>Blessed be Creative Flame in the darkness.
>
>Blessed be songwriters and musicians who lead us to think.
>
>Blessed be the "crack that lets the light in".
>
>Blessed be agents of change in a sometimes-hostile world.
>
>Blessed be Creative Flame, flowing through me in ever surprising ways.
>
>Blessed be Infinite Beauty, flowing in me that I may live freely, happily and justly.
>
>Blessed be Beauty before me.
>
>Blessed be Beauty behind me.
>
>Blessed be Beauty below me.
>
>Blessed be Beauty above me.
>
>Blessed be Beauty.

Conclude with one minute of contemplative silence.

Fire ~ West ~ Autumn ~ Beauty

WAY OF BEAUTY

"There is something about deep space, about the magnitude of our galaxy and the billions of spiralling clusters of stars that is evocative of a silence that is primordial and eternal. Surely there is a pattern there that not only reflects the beauty of God but invites us to enter into that pattern, to become one with what is reflected." (Colleen Rhodes RSM 'Trinity: Heart of the Cosmic Mystery' in ISMAPNG website)

Song: *Beauty Before Me* Jeff Stockton –streaming Apple Music and Spotify.

Begin with three minutes of contemplative silence and Acknowledgment of Country.

Listen to the song.

I experienced an example of the *Way of Beauty* when I received this poem from a friend who was visiting Balgo in the Great Sandy Desert, Western Australia. The closest town is a five-hour drive on a very rough road.

Sit with both feet on the floor. Allow the chair you are sitting in to support your back. Play *Beauty before Me.*

Become aware of the sound of the music playing softly in the background. Listen to the melody and begin to pay attention to your breathing. Close your eyes and meditate for 2 minutes.

Read: The Way of Beauty

> A sky strewn full of stars…
> early morning moon a quarter way on her course…
>
> the first light… deepening colours of the desert in the east and in the west soft pink and blue. On and on into wonder!
>
> The painted beauty of the Balgo hills… brush stroked from the ancient inland sea…a moment in timelessness…
>
> climbing down the rocks great walls of ochre red stone leading to water waiting for rains to move further… rock painting of the life story of before…
> a glimpse of one hundred brolgas… reminding me of the carol that out on the plains the brolgas are dancing!
>
> bush tomato, cockroach bush, tiny green lichen like plants on the track bursting with delicate flower… red earth… red sand hills.
>
> (Helen Densley used with permission.)

Take a few moments to remember some of your experiences of beauty. Bring them to mind and breathe in and out with gratitude.

May I walk in beauty, beauty beside me, beauty behind me, beauty ahead of me, beauty above me, and beauty below me. May I be aware of beauty!

Conclude with one minute of contemplative silence.

Fire ~ West ~ Autumn ~ Beauty

WAY OF BLESSING AND AFFIRMATION: A MEDITATION WITH OILS

"**Each celebration should encourage men and women to become more aware of the fruitfulness, beauty, abundance and yet extraordinary fragility of earth. Liturgies that use the symbols of sun, earth, water, food, light, darkness, moon and sky should celebrate the story of the cosmos and call attention to the cosmic damage now taking place.**" (Sean McDonagh 1986:158)

A bowl of oil is prepared beforehand and placed in the setting with a cloth and candle.
Begin with three minutes of contemplative silence and Acknowledgment of Country.
Song: *Could it Be* Jan Novotka – streaming on Apple Music and Spotify.

Could it be? Could it be? Could it be that the Universe could see?
Could it be that it is self-aware?
Could it be you and me are the consciousness of the Universe?

Could it be? Could it be that this consciousness comes from Mystery?
From the Source of all Life and all things?
Could it be you and me are the consciousness of mystery?

Could it be? Could it be that Mystery's the Ground of all Being?
Energy pulsing with Sacred Power?
Could it be you and me are the consciousness of the Ground of Being?

© 2006 by Jan Novotka's Music, LLC (ASCAP). All rights reserved.

After listening to the song, there is a brief reflection meditation in silence with an attitude of gratitude for the cosmos.

Read the quote above and recall the Story of the Universe and the damage happening on earth right now.

Aware of the mystery of all that is, inspired by Source of all Life, we open our hearts to the question "Could it be?" We lament earth degradation and lack of consciousness about the cosmic story.

The oil becomes for us a sign of sustenance and nourishment as we ponder this mystery.
If you are doing this ritual by yourself, use the oil to bless yourself.
If you are doing this ritual with others, anoint the person on your right on the forehead, cheeks and hands.
Play: "Could it be?"
Conclude with one minute of contemplative silence.

Fire ~ West ~ Autumn ~ Beauty

AN AUTUMN MANDALA

"The earth is set firmly in its place and cannot be moved. The trees in the forest will shout for joy." (Psalm 96:10)

(A circular tablecloth is placed on the floor and the group is invited to gather autumn leaves from outside and then return to the room.)

Song: *Circle Round* Murray Kyle https://murraykyle.bandcamp.com/track/circle-round

Begin with three minutes of contemplative silence and Acknowledgment of Country.

Leader: We give thanks for all that is, leaves of the universe raising our awareness now, honouring connectedness.

The Leaf: Thich Nhat Hanh

"I asked the leaf whether it was frightened because it was autumn and the other leaves were falling. The leaf told me, 'No. During the whole spring and summer I was completely alive. I worked hard to help nourish the tree, and now much of me is in the tree. I am not limited by this form. I am also the whole tree, and when I go back to the soil, I will continue to nourish the tree. So I don't worry at all. As I leave this branch and float to the ground, I will wave to the tree and tell her, 'I will see you again very soon.'

"You have to see life. You should not say, life of the leaf, you should only speak of life in the leaf and life in the tree. My life is just Life, and you can see it in me and in the tree. That day there was a wind blowing and, after a while, I saw the leaf leave the branch and float down to the soil, dancing joyfully, because as it floated it saw itself already there in the tree. It was so happy. I bowed my head, knowing that I have a lot to learn from the leaf because it is not afraid – it knew nothing can be born and nothing can die."

After this reading, the leaves are placed on the cloth in silence to create the autumn mandala.

When the mandala is complete all gather in a circle and contemplate in silence.

Movement: Stand in a circle around the finished mandala and step moving to the right, keeping with the rhythm of the song *Circle Round*.

Each one then picks up an edge of the mandala cloth and allows the leaves to fall into the centre. These will now be returned to earth and form compost for the next season.

Echo of Gratitude:
- We give thanks for all that is.   All repeat.
- Leaves of the universe now.   All repeat.
- Knowing our interconnectedness.   All repeat.

Conclude the ritual outside with one minute of contemplative silence.

Fire ~ West ~ Autumn ~ Beauty

BLESSING OF THE ANIMALS SUNDAY

"Ask the animals and they will teach you. Ask the birds of the air and they will teach you." (Job 12:7-10)

(Adapted with permission http://normanhabel.com/)

Begin with three minutes of contemplative silence and Acknowledgment of Country.

'Animals' refers to all the living beings in the community of life, from microbes in soil, to worms, insects, fish, birds, and reptiles, mammals, domesticated or wild. People may wish to bring a picture of an animal they love, such as a pet or an endangered species in the wild. Acknowledging that humans are part of the profoundly related animal community, in this ritual, we honour and pray for the other-than-human community.

Setting: This ritual may be best held outdoors in a park, a garden or the bush where other-than-human beings can be experienced. Banners or artworks with animals may also be used indoors.

Gathering

Leader: We come together with all creatures in this circle of life, radiant with the divine mystery of love.

Response: We celebrate as one!

Leader: We awaken to the sacred presence and creative, emergent unfolding in all beings.

Response: We celebrate as one!

Leader: We continue to open our hearts to the blessings we receive from each one in this great family of relatedness.

Response: We celebrate as one!

Circle of Praise: A Version of Psalm 148

Leader: All dogs and dingoes, large and small:

Response: Praise the ground of our being!

Leader: All rabbits, hamsters and guinea pigs:

Response: Praise the ground of our being!

Leader: All goldfish, guppies and swimming creatures:

Response: Praise the ground of our being!

Leader: All kookaburras, budgies and singing birds:

Response: Praise the ground of our being!

Leader: All wombats, koalas and wallabies:

Response: **Praise the ground of our being!**

Leader: All horses, cows and sheep:

Response: **Praise the ground of our being!**

Leader: All lizards, skinks and crawling creatures:

Response: **Praise the ground of our being!**

Leader: Every animal in the sky, the sea and the forest:

Response: **Praise the ground of our being!**

We Give Thanks and Lament Litany

Leader: Blessed be Source of all life, for all the animals in the whole wide world,

> **Blessed be**

Leader: Blessed be all the fun and friendship we have with animals,

> **Blessed be**

Leader: We lament all the times we have hurt or neglected animals,

> **We lament**

Leader: We lament all the times we have used poisons that have killed animals,

> **We lament**

Leader: We lament all the times we have destroyed the homes of animals in the forests, oceans, fields, towns and cities.

> **We lament**

Invocation

Living Mystery,
You draw us toward deeper communion with all beings, to love all creatures as kin; to relate to the animals of Earth as our companions in life and lead us to celebrate our place in the circle of life; to experience all animals as partners with humans on Earth; all birds as messengers of the sacred; all minute beings as expressions of mysterious design; and all frogs as voices of hope. Amen.

Conclude with one minute of contemplative silence.

Fire ~ West ~ Autumn ~ Beauty

THE IN BETWEEN LIGHT

"**This world, in which we are born and take our being, is alive. It is not our supply house and sewer. It is our larger body. The intelligence that evolved us from stardust, and interconnects us with all beings, is sufficient for the healing of our Earth community.**" **(Joanna Macy, Molly Young Brown 2014:66)**

Begin with three minutes of contemplative silence followed by Acknowledgment of Country.

Sufi Fire Breath: Relax, breathing your natural breath. As you do the breath for the fire element, attune your heartbeat and experience the energy pulsing through your body.

Inhale through the mouth and exhale through the nose.
Repeat this Fire Breath five times.

Leader: Today we will adapt *Lectio Divina* to reflect on this poem by Helen Densley (used with permission) and as we gather in this circle let us listen to a reading of the poem.

"*Lectio Divina...* is an ancient practice and can include any sacred text – a passage that moves you, a poem you love, or an image that is calling for your attention." (Christine Valters Paintner 2011:18)

The In Between Light

> I see a light
> at dusk
> at dawn
> at the moment
> in between the rain
> and the sun setting
> and the rainbow
>
> I see a light
> I catch my breath
> in this moment
> of crisp wintering
> as autumn reds and golds
> lift up in counter tenor
> with grey clouds
> in the intensity
> of the song of the universe
> I am one
> with the in-between-light

Leader: Let us listen to the poem as it is read again and this time you will be invited to share one word that stays with you.

Fire ~ West ~ Autumn ~ Beauty

Circle sharing with pauses to allow slowing down, becoming fully present, and maintaining a sense of awe and wonder as each one speaks. There is no discussion. Listen actively. There is no rush. Slowly and mindfully contemplatively listen.

Leader: Let us listen to the poem for a third time and you are asked to listen for an invitation that stays with you.

The In Between Light

> I see a light
> at dusk
> at dawn
> at the moment
> in between the rain
> and the sun setting
> and the rainbow
>
> I see a light
> I catch my breath
> in this moment
> of crisp wintering
> as autumn reds and golds
> lift up in counter tenor
> with grey clouds
> in the intensity
> of the song of the universe
> I am one
> with the in-between-light

Circle sharing with pauses to allow slowing down, becoming fully present, and maintaining a sense of awe and wonder as each one speaks. There is no discussion. Listen actively. There is no rush. Slowly and mindfully contemplatively listen.

What is the invitation of this poem?
What stays with me?
What is present?
Move into groups of three.

Group Sharing: Share your favourite images and metaphors from this poem and what you are being invited to allow emerge in your own life.

To conclude the groups return to one large circle and sit in silence.

Leader: Let us now breathe the Sufi Fire Breath together. Inhale through the mouth and exhale through the nose. Do this breath five times.

Conclude with one minute of contemplative silence.

Fire ~ West ~ Autumn ~ Beauty

EARTH DAY

2020 will mark Earth Day's 50th Anniversary! As the global coordinator of Earth Day, Earth Day Network is working to make sure that Earth Day 2020 is the most diverse global mobilisation in defence of the environment in world history. We work year-round with more than 50,000 partner organisations in 190 countries, and our global campaigns and programs bring hundreds of thousands of new voices – representing youth and faculty, the faith community, minority groups, women, teachers, students and others – into the environmental movement. The opportunity is before us now to use the 50th anniversary of Earth Day as a catalytic event to reignite the environmental movement and unite the vast array of groups and individuals who care for and protect the earth. (https://www.earthday.org/earthday/countdown-to-2020/)

Everyone invited is asked to bring a bunch of herbs to this ritual.

Symbols of earth and the herbs are placed into the centre of the circle on a cloth already prepared.

Begin with three minutes of contemplative silence and Acknowledgment of Country.

Play the Song: *Every Moment* Murray Kyle https://murraykyle.bandcamp.com/track/every-moment

Meditation: Each person picks up their bunch of herbs and smells the fragrance. Slowly the herbs are passed around the circle and each time there is a pause to inhale the herb's fragrance.

A Litany of Earth (adapted from Chief Seattle's Speech). One person reads and everyone responds.

Tenderness flows through me now; connecting to all that is; healing all and spreading love.

Every part of earth is sacred.

Tenderness flows through me now; connecting to all that is; healing all and spreading love.

Every clearing and every insect is holy.

Tenderness flows through me now; connecting to all that is; healing all and spreading love.

Whatever befalls the earth befalls the children of earth.

Tenderness flows through me now; connecting to all that is; healing all and spreading love.

We are part of earth and earth is part of us.

Tenderness flows through me now; connecting to all that is; healing all and spreading love.

The rivers are our brothers; they quench our thirst; the perfumed flowers are our sisters; the air is precious; this we know – earth does not belong to us; we belong to earth.

Tenderness flows through me now; connecting to all that is; healing all and spreading love.

Conclude with one minute of contemplative silence.

Fire ~ West ~ Autumn ~ Beauty

BIBLICAL PRAYERS (ADAPTED)

"Let your soul, your heart, be folded into the Holy One so that nothing at all will keep the world's sweetness from you." (Jon M. Sweeney & Mark S. Burrows 2017:94)

Begin with three minutes of contemplative silence and Acknowledgment of Country.

Breathe in fresh air and light a candle to focus on whilst you read and pray these prayers meditatively.

Our Father Adapted at a workshop by Pat O'Gorman, Gabrielle Sinclair and Loretta Brinkman. (Rahamim Ecology Centre Bathurst 2019)

Source of Life, embodied in the whole evolving cosmos.
Blessed beyond all names.
Creator, animator, leaven and liberating communion for all of creation,
let the transforming table of our hospitality be wide,
empowering mercy and compassion as we respond
to the cry of earth and the cry of the poor.
We go and do likewise. Amen.

O Cosmic Source of Wisdom,
protector and provider, embracing all that dwells.
Naming all as sacred and just.
In the companionship of empowerment,
amongst evolving creation, the reflection of holy wisdom is present.
In justice may all be sustained by daily bread,
as we respond to the cry of earth and the cry of the poor.
We awaken to peace.
May we live in peace in harmony
and reject all forms of oppression.
We commit to radiate enduring hope. Amen.

Blessed be those who know everything is gift; for within is the pearl of great price.
Blessed are those who mourn for the degradation of earth and cosmic pain; for within is true compassion.
Blessed are the risk-takers, the bold adventurers who seek justice; for within is the power of courage and commitment.
Blessed are the truth seekers; for within is unlimited courage and communion.
Blessed are the compassionate who cry and lament the world injustice; for within is Divine Presence.
Blessed are those who reverence all that is and reverence inter-connections; for within is Divine Mystery.
Blessed are those who love for love's sake; for within is Loving Mystery ever present. (Adapted by author)

Conclude with one minute of contemplative silence.

Fire ~ West ~ Autumn ~ Beauty

CELEBRATING EIGHTH WORK OF MERCY

"…may the works of mercy also include care for our common home? As a spiritual work of mercy, care for our common home calls for a 'grateful contemplation of God's world'. (LS: 214) *As a corporal work of mercy, care for our common home requires 'simple daily gestures which break with the logic of violence, exploitation and selfishness' and 'makes itself felt in every action that seeks to build a better world".* (LS: 230) (Pope Francis issued from the Vatican September 1st 2016.)

Song: *May all Beings* One Love Devotional Chant – streaming on Apple Music and Spotify.

Begin with three minutes of contemplative silence followed by Acknowledgment of Country.

Read this direction first and then… place your left hand over your heart and close your eyes.

Listen to your heartbeat as you breathe in and out in the silence. (Allow one to two minutes.) Now, please place your right hand over your left hand and put your thumbs together and place the soles of your feet on the floor. We are connected to the earth and conscious of our heart beating. We are calling to mind the celebration of the eighth work of mercy caring for our common home.

Read one line at a time and breathe in the prayer:
May I be filled with loving kindness.
May I be peaceful and at ease.
May I be well? May I be happy.   *Pause*

May all beings be filled with loving kindness.
May all beings be peaceful and at ease.
May all beings be well.
May all beings be happy.   *Pause*

Play *May all Beings*, keep your eyes closed and your hands over your heart.

When the song finishes, stand and face the direction of the west. The west holds the element fire, the season autumn and the gift of beauty.

With your hands extended to the west, pray:
May all beings be filled with loving kindness.
May all beings be peaceful and at ease.
May all beings be well.
May all beings be happy.

May all beings be filled with loving kindness, compassion and unconditional love.
May all beings know healing presence and peace in the midst of chaos.
May all beings be peaceful and at ease.
May all beings be well and happy.

Conclude with one minute of contemplative silence.

Fire ~ West ~ Autumn ~ Beauty

COSMIC SPARKS

"It is time to embrace… the essential embodied nature of life – personal, planetary and cosmic alike. All embodied forms coexist interdependently and are the primary vehicles for the manifestation and transmission of the creative power of Spirit. Embodiment is the primary realm in which creative transformation takes place, and we witness that in a unique way in Eucharistic celebrations… It is time to outgrow…the patriarchal alienation around the body… we have largely forgotten the cosmic womb from which we and every species evolves." **(Diarmuid O'Murchu 2003:137)**

Song: *Walk Lightly*-streaming Apple Music and Spotify.

When Diarmuid O'Murchu asks readers to consider the importance of the evolutionary story as an unfolding story into the future, there is an implication that this needs time for reflection and the letting go of some of the old stories. This ritual invites you to go for a long walk with the intention to ponder in your heart the words of the song *Walk Lightly* and the quotations from O'Murchu (above).

You will need this book outside.

Begin with three minutes of contemplative silence and Acknowledgment of Country.

Walk slowly and lightly outside; feel the sun; see the clouds; hear the birds; feel the breeze.

Play the song as you walk.

Stop by a nearby rock or seat and slowly read the words of the song:

Touch the sea. Feel the sun. Walk lightly as you go.
Know the land. Love the Earth. Walk lightly as you go.
　　　　　　　© *2006 by Jan Novotka's Music, LLC (ASCAP). All rights reserved.*

Silently Pray

Great Spirit is with me; flowing within me; igniting a re-enchantment with the sacred.

I experience beauty as I walk. I am grateful for this gift.

I am inspired by others who have walked this path of truth and justice.

Clouds and fire, *Cosmic Sparks* re-enchant me; call me to inner reflection on all that is.

I go forth today and tomorrow with open eyes to see the 'spark' of Great Spirit present in all I meet and in all I see. Amen.

Conclude with one minute of contemplative silence.

BIBLIOGRAPHY

Abram, David. *Becoming Animal: An Earthly Cosmology*. Penguin Random House 2010

Berry, Thomas 2001: "Ecozoic Activism" Earthlight 42:33 2001

Berry, Thomas. *Creative Energy*. Sierra Club Pathstone 1988

Berry, Thomas. *The Christian Future and the Fate of the Earth*. Ed. Mary Evelyn Tucker and John Grim. Maryknoll, NY: Orbis Books, 2009.

Berry Thomas *The Dream of the Earth* Sierra Books 1988, reprinted 1990

Berry, Thomas. *The Great Work*. NYP: Bell Tower, 1999

Boff Leonardo. *The Path to Hope*. Orbis Books, 1993.

Boyd, Anne. 'From the editor' *Earthsong Journal* 2009

Boyd Anne 'Chaos and Creativity', *Earthsong Journal* 2013

Cannato Judy *Field of Compassion: How the New Cosmology is Transforming Spiritual Life*, Sorin Books 2010

Cannato Judy *Radical Amazement: Contemplative Lessons from Black Holes, Supernovas, and Other Wonders of the Universe*, Sorin Books 2006

Carson, Rachel *Silent Spring* Penguin Books 1962

Chittister, Joan *The Breath of the Soul: Reflections on Prayer* Garrett Publishing 2009

Christian, David *Origin Story: A Big History of Everything* Penguin Random House UK 2018

Cleary, William *Prayers to an Evolutionary God* Sky Paths Publishing 2004

De Chardin, Teilhard *Hymn of the Universe* William Collins Sons & Co Ltd 1961

Delio, Ilia, ed. *Personal Transformation and a New Creation: The Spiritual Revolution of Beatrice Bruteau* Orbis Books 2017

Delio, Ilia *the Unbearable Wholeness of Being: God, Evolution and the Power of Love* Orbis Books 2013

Dellinger, Drew *Love Letters to the Milky Way: A Book of Poems* White Cloud Press, 2011

Dorr, Donal 'From Vatican 11 to Laudato Si' in *Laudato Si' an Irish Response: Essays on the Pope's Letter on the Environment* Veritas 2017

Dowd, Michael and Barlow, Connie 'Ecozoic Activism' *Earthlight* 2001

Edwards, Denis *Ecology at the Heart of Faith* Orbis Books 2006

Edwards, Denis *Made from Stardust* CollinsDove 1992

Fabel, Arthur, St John, Donald eds. *Teilhard in the 21st Century: The Emerging Spirit of Earth* Orbis Books 2003

Faulkner, Peter 'A Journey into the Flinders Ranges' *Earthsong* Autumn 2005

Feehan, John *The Singing Heart of the World* Orbis Books 2012

Flannery, Tim *Atmosphere of Hope* Penguin Books, London 2015

Fox, Matthew *Naming the Unnameable: 89 Wonderful and Useful Names for God* Little Bound Books 2018

Habel, Norman C. *Seven Songs of Creation: Liturgies for Celebrating and Healing Earth* The Pilgrim Press 2004

Hahn, Thich Nhat *Love Letter to the Earth* Parallax Press 2013

Hahn, Thich Nhat *The Miracle of Mindfulness* Beacon Press Books 1975

Harvey, Andrew *The Hope: A Guide to Sacred Activism* Carlsbard United States 2009

Haught, John F. *Resting on the Future: Catholic Theology for an Unfinished Universe* Bloomsbury 2015

Haught, John F. *The New Cosmic Story: Inside Our Awakening Universe* Yale University Press 2017

Higgins, Carmel *Heart and Mind of Cosmos* Carmel Higgins 2018

Howard, Adele rsm ed. *Mercy International Reflection Process Guide Book.* 2018

Huebsch, Bill, Hindmarsh, Trish *Care for Our Common Home: An Australian Group Reading Guide to Pope Francis' Laudato Si'* Garratt Publishing 2015

Johnson, Elizabeth A *Abounding in Kindness: Writings for the People of God* Orbis Books 2015

Johnson, Elizabeth A *Ask the Beasts: Darwin and the God of Love* Bloomsbury Publishing 2014

Johnson, Elizabeth A *Creation and the Cross: The Mercy of God for a Planet in Peril* Orbis Books 2018

Johnstone, Chris 'Seeing With New Eyes: How to Practice Active Hope' *Resurgence Ecologist* March/April 2014

Jorna, Dave 'Climbing the Mountain' *Australian Catholics* Winter 2019

June, Raymond (ed.) *Meditations with Thomas Berry*, Greensprint, 2010

Kauffman, Stuart *At Home in the Universe: The search for the Laws of Self-Organization and Complexity* Oxford University Press 1995

Kelley, Kevin *The Home Planet* Addison-Wesley 1988

Klein, Naomi *This Changes Everything: Capitalism vs The Climate* Simon & Schuster 2014

Klotz, Neil-Douglas *Blessings of the Cosmos: Wisdom of the Heart from the Aramaic Words of Jesus* Sounds True 2006

Klotz, Neil-Douglas *Prayers of the Cosmos* Harper One 1990

Kureethadam, Joshtrom Isaac *The Ten Green Commandments of Laudato Si'* Liturgical Press 2019

Lawson, Veronica M *The Blessings of Mercy: Biblical Perspectives and Ecological Challenges* Morning Star Publishing 2015

Livingstone, Glenys *PaGaian Cosmology* Universe Books 2005, reprinted 2008.

Lonergan, A. and Richards, C. eds 1998. *Thomas Berry and the New Cosmology* 2nd ed. CT: Twenty-Third publications.

Long, Pat 'Eating Mindfully' *Earthsong Journal* Autumn 2009

Macy Joanna, Brown Molly Young, *Coming Back to Life: practices to Reconnect our Lives, Our world.* New Society Publishers 1998

Macy Joanna, Brown Molly Young, *Coming Back to Life: The Updated Guide to the Work that Reconnects* New Society Publishers 2014

Macy Joanna, Johnstone, Chris *Active Hope: How to Face the Mess We are in without Going Crazy* New World Library 2012

Manifold, Philomena *Written in Stone: Reading the Rocks of The Great Ocean Road* Philomena Manifold 2017

McDonagh Sean *To Care For the Earth; a call to a new theology* Geoffrey Chapman 1986

McDonagh, Sean ed. *Laudato Si' an Irish Response: Essays on the Pope's Letter on the Environment* Veritas 2017

McDonagh, Sean *Laudato Si'* Orbis Books, 2015

McIntyre, Margaret *The Cosmic Pilgrim* Wipf and Stock 2010

McLaughlin, Nellie *Life's Delicate Balance: Our Common Home & Laudato Si'* Veritas 2015

McLaughlin, Nellie *Out of Wonder: the Evolving Story of the Universe* Veritas 2004

Merton, Thomas *Selected Poems of Thomas Merton* NY: New Directions 1967

Merrill, Nan C *Psalms for Praying: An Invitation to Wholeness* Bloomsbury Publishing 2007

Morwood, Michael *Prayers for Progressive Christians* Kelmore Publications 2018

Morwood, Michael *Praying a New Story* Spectrum 2003

Muir, John *The Yosemite* Biblio Press 2007

Neu, Diann L *Return Blessings: Ecofeminist Liturgies renewing the earth* Wild Goose Publications 2002

Newell, John Philip *The Rebirthing of God* Skylight Paths Publishing 2014

Nguyen Anh-Huong & Thich Nhat Hahn *Walking Meditation* Sounds True 2006

Okuizumi H *The Stones Cry Out* Harcourt Brace 2000

O'Leary, Daniel *An Astonishing Secret: The Love story of Creation and the Wonder of You* Garratt Publishing 2017

O'Leary, Daniel *Dancing to My Death: With the Love Called Cancer* Garratt Publishing 2019

O'Leary, Daniel *Passion for the Possible* Columba Press 1998

O'Leary, Daniel *The Healing Habit* Columba Press 2016

O'Murchu, Diarmuid *Ancestral Grace* Orbis Books 2008

O'Murchu, Diarmuid *Evolutionary Faith* Orbis Books 2003

O'Murchu, Diarmuid *In the Beginning was the Spirit: Science, Religion, and Indigenous Spirituality* Orbis Books 2012

O'Murchu, Diarmuid *Incarnation: A New Evolutionary Threshold* Orbis Books 2017

O'Murchu, Diarmuid *Reclaiming Spirituality* Gill &Macmillan 1997

Paintner, Christine Valters *The Artist's Rule: Nurturing Your Creative Soul with Monastic Wisdom* Sorin Books 2011

Paintner, Christine Valters *Water, Wind, Earth & Fire: the Christian Practice of Praying with the Elements* Sorin Books 2010

Paintner, Christine Valters, *The Soul's Slow Ripening* Sorin Books 2018

Parton, Trevor *A Sense of Place* (Blog, May 2019).

Parton, Trevor *Fire, Earth, Air and Water: poems, Images and Essays on Ecology, Cosmology & Spirituality* Brougham Press 2017

Primavesi, Anne *Sacred Gaia* Routledge 2000

Pope Francis *Laudato Si* Rome 2015

Roberts, Elizabeth Amidon, Elias *Earth Prayers from around the World* HarperSanFrancisco 1991

Rohr, Richard *The Universal Christ: How a Forgotten Reality Can Change Everything We See, Hope for and Believe* Convergent Books 2019

Ross, Gillian *Consciousness v Catastrophe: Reflections on the Next Stage of Human Evolution* XLibris 2016

Rowthorn, Anne ed. *Earth and all the Stars: Reconnecting with Nature through Hymns, Stories, poems, and Prayers from the World's Great Religions and Cultures.* Resource Publications 2000

Rue, Charles *Eucharist and Laudato Si: Care for Our Common Home* Columban's Missions 2017

Silf, Margaret *The Way of Wisdom* Lion Hudson 2006

Suzuki, David with McConnell, Amanda *The Sacred Balance: Rediscovering Our Place in Nature* Allen and Unwin 1997

Sweeney, Jon M & Burrows, Mark S *Meister Eckhart's Book of the Heart: Meditations for the Restless Soul* Hampton Roads Publishing Company, Inc. Charlottesville VA 2017

Swimme, Brian *The Universe is a Green Dragon* Bear & Co, Inc. 1984

Swimme, Brian *The Hidden Heart of the Cosmos: Humanity and the New Story* Orbis Books 1996

Swimme, Brian Thomas Tucker & Mary Evelyn *Journey of the Universe* Yale University Press 2011

Szirom, Tricia *Seasons of the Goddess: Perspectives from the Southern Hemisphere* Gaia's Garden 2011

Tacey David 'Ecological Awareness as Initiation' *Earthsong Journal*, 2016.

Toolan, David *At Home in the Cosmos*, Orbis Books 2001

Treston, Kevin *Walk Lightly Upon the Earth* Creation Enterprises 2003kevin

Treston, Kevin *Who do You Say that I am: the Christ story in the Cosmic Context?* Morning Star Publishing 2016

Uhlein, Gabriele (ed.) *Meditations of Hildegard of Bingen.* Santa Fe, NM Bear & Co., 1982

Washington Haydn *Healing the Planet through Belonging* Routledge 2018

Wessels, Cletus *The Holy Web: Church and the New Universe Story* Orbis Books 2000

Wohlleben, Peter *The Hidden Life of Trees: What they Feel and How They Communicate* Black Inc., 2016

Worcelo, Gail 'Discovering the Divine within the Universe' *Earthlight* 39:2000

www.ingramcontent.com/pod-product-compliance
Lightning Source LLC
Chambersburg PA
CBHW060522010526
44107CB00060B/2653